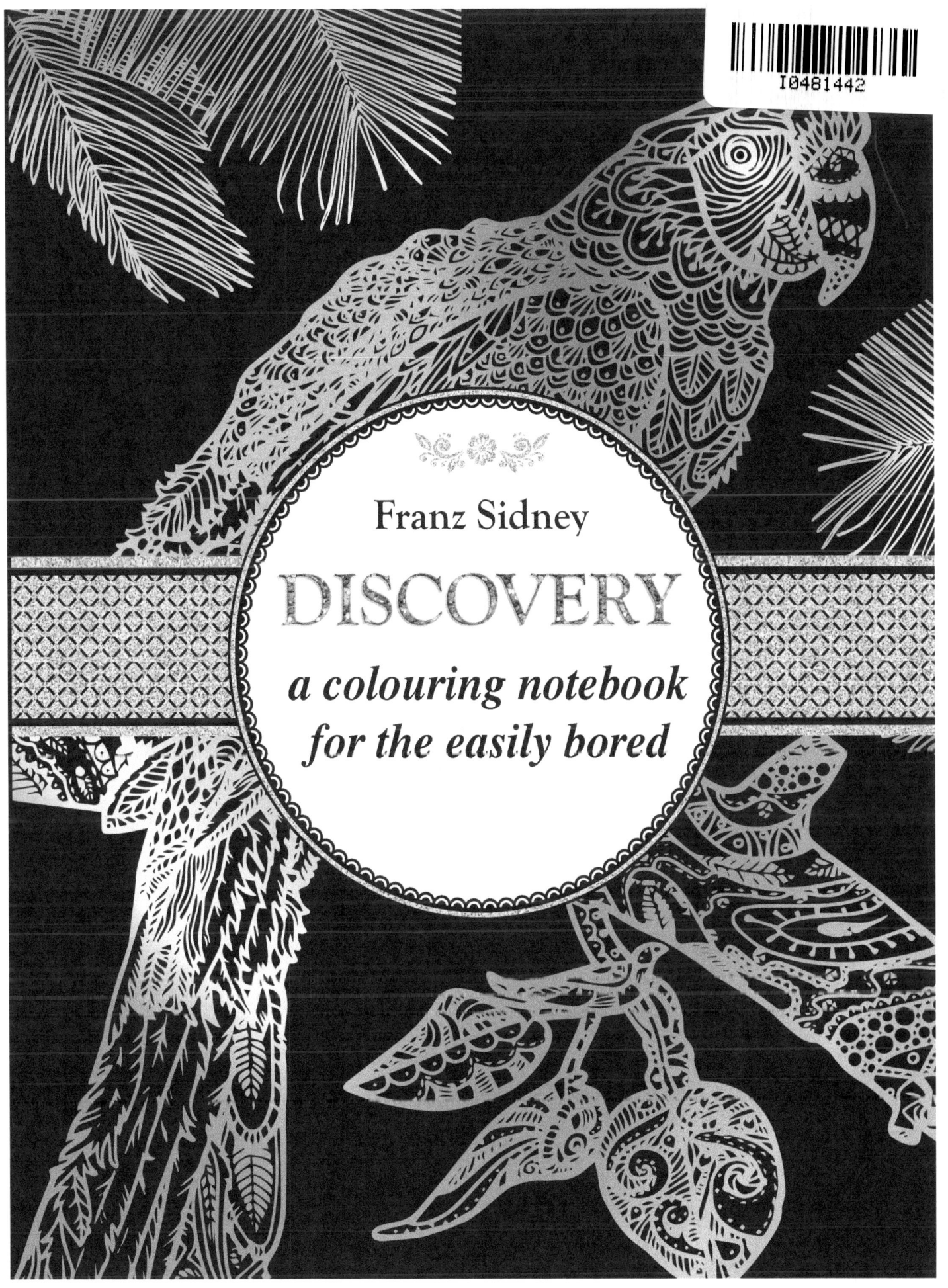

Franz Sidney

DISCOVERY

*a colouring notebook
for the easily bored*

THIS COLOURING NOTEBOOK BELONGS TO:

_____

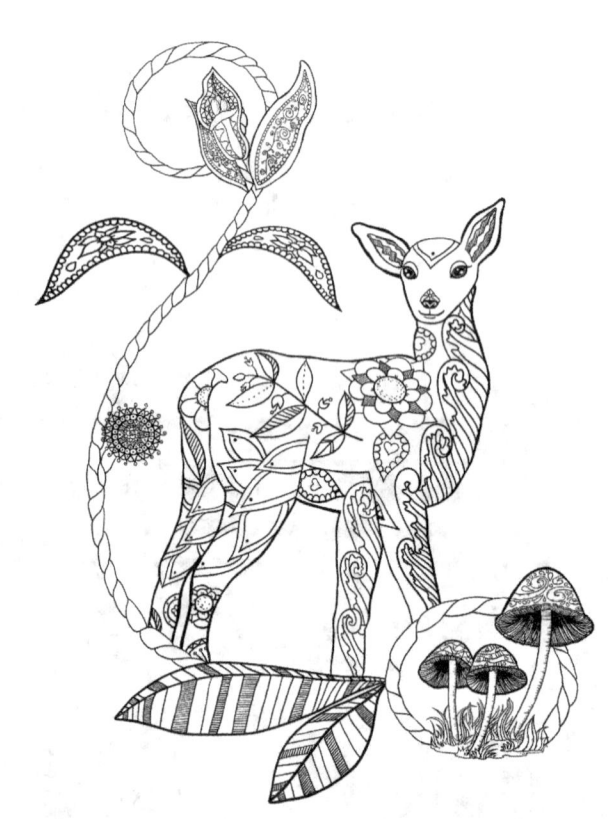

MY YEARLY GOALS

GOALS THIS WEEK	ACTIONS	COMPLETED

"NO ONE HAS EVER BECOME POOR BY GIVING."
DIARY OF ANNE FRANK

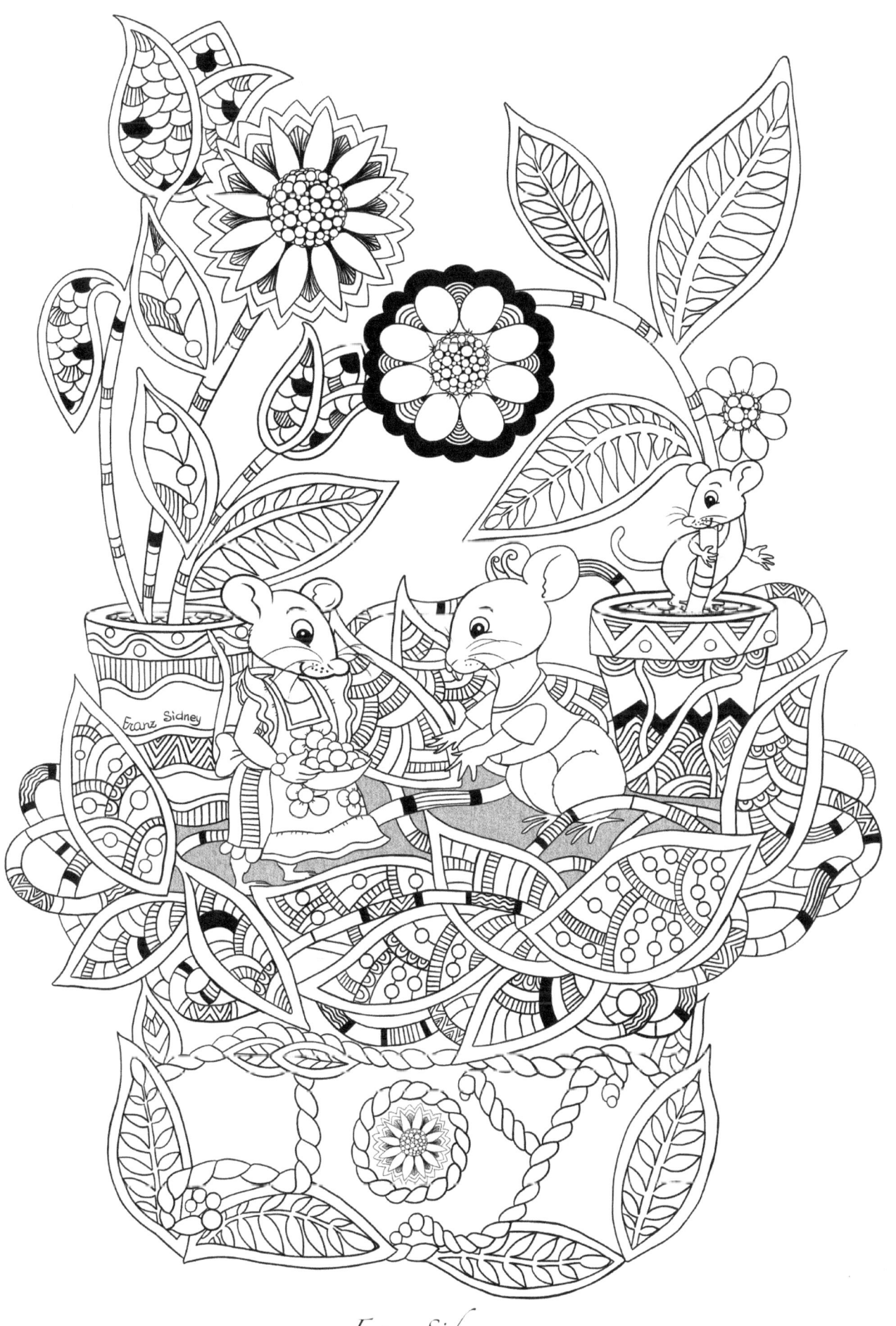

Franz Sidney

"HAPPINESS IS LIKE A BUTTERFLY WHICH, WHEN PURSUED, IS ALWAYS BEYOND OUR GRASP, BUT, IF YOU WILL SIT DOWN QUIETLY, MAY ALIGHT UPON YOU."
NATHANIEL HAWTHORNE

_____

_____

_____

_____

_____

_____

_____

_____

_____

_____

_____

_____

_____

_____

_____

_____

_____

_____

_____

_____

_____

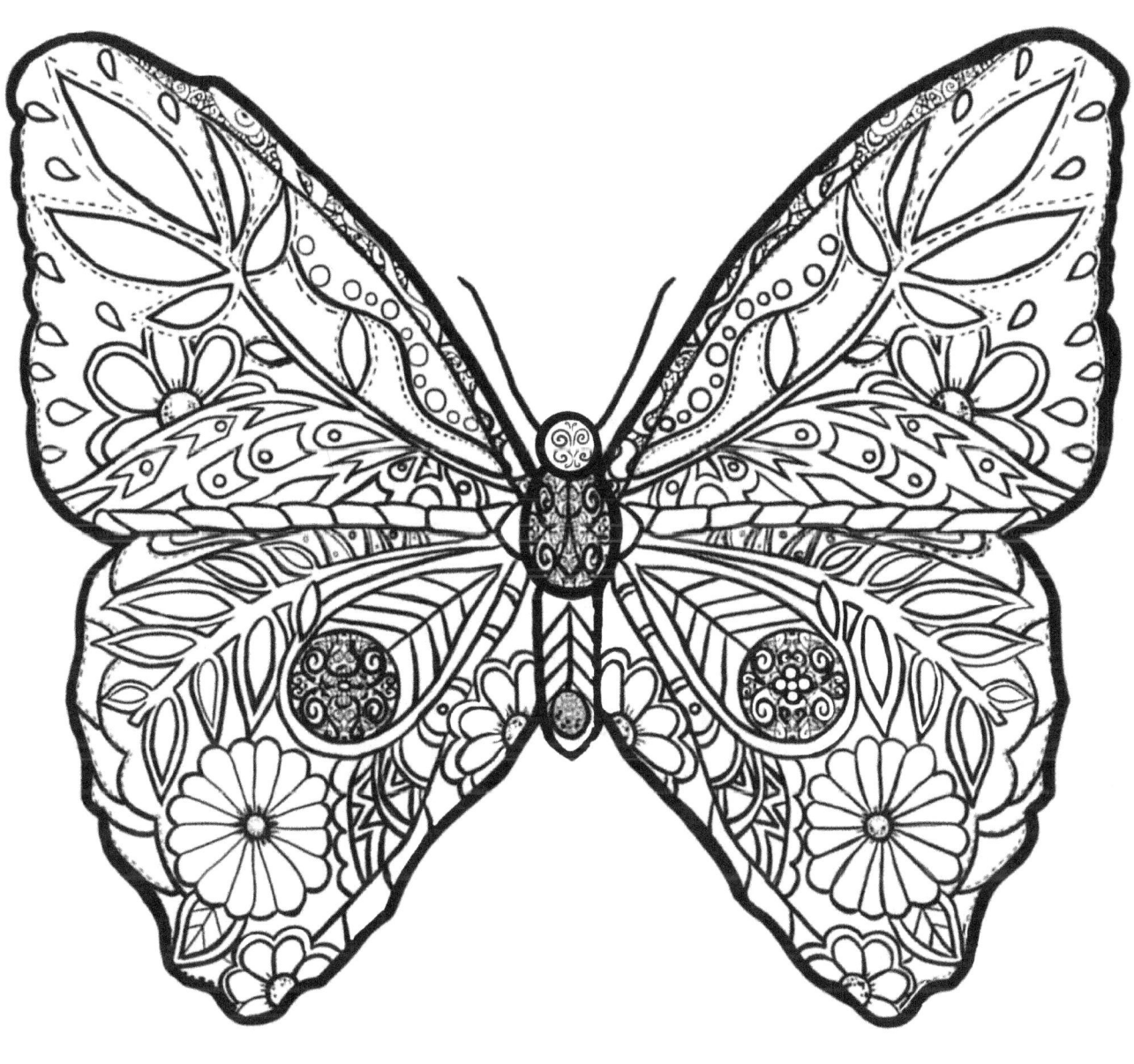

"A DOG IS THE ONLY THING ON EARTH THAT LOVES YOU MORE THAN HE LOVES HIMSELF."
JOSH BILLINGS

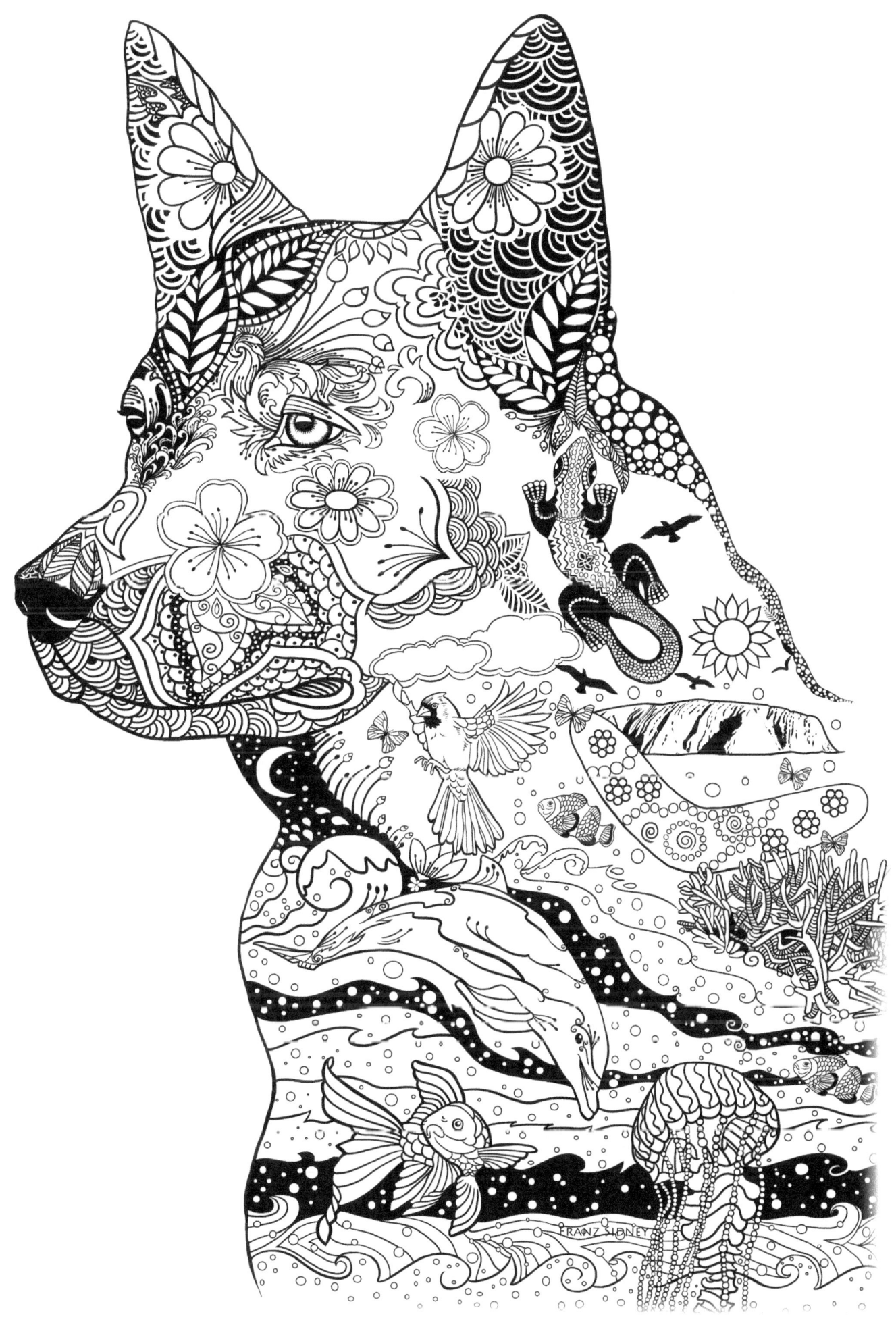

> "I WANT TO SING LIKE THE BIRDS SING, NOT WORRYING ABOUT WHO HEARS OR WHAT THEY THINK."
> JALALUDDIN RUMI

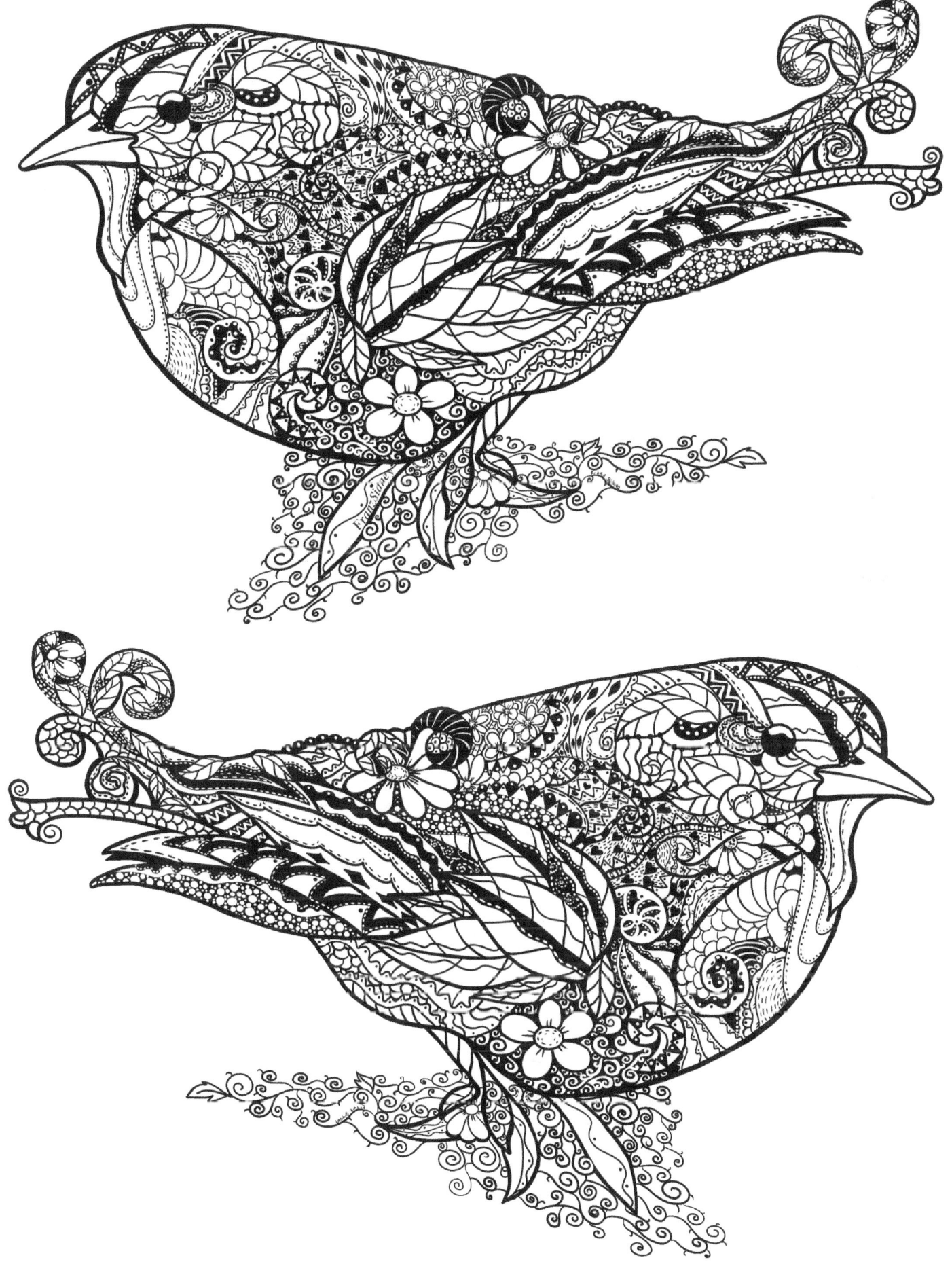

"THE FLOWER THAT BLOOMS IN ADVERSITY IS THE RAREST AND MOST BEAUTIFUL OF ALL."
WALT DISNEY COMPANY, MULAN

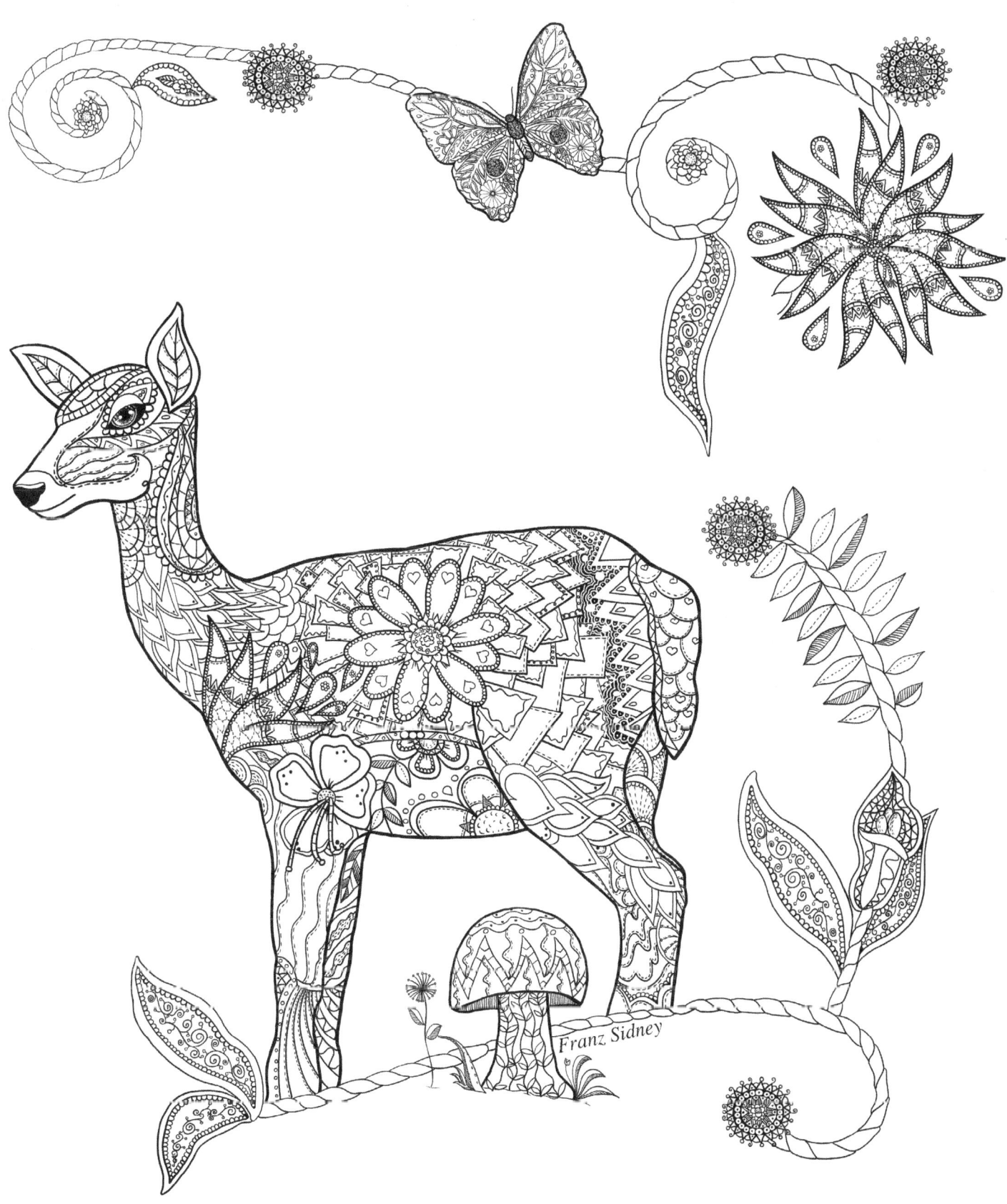

Franz Sidney

"MONSTERS ARE REAL, AND GHOSTS ARE REAL TOO.
THEY LIVE INSIDE US, AND SOMETIMES, THEY WIN."
STEPHEN KING

_____

_____

_____

_____

_____

_____

_____

_____

_____

_____

_____

_____

_____

_____

_____

_____

_____

_____

_____

_____

_____

_____

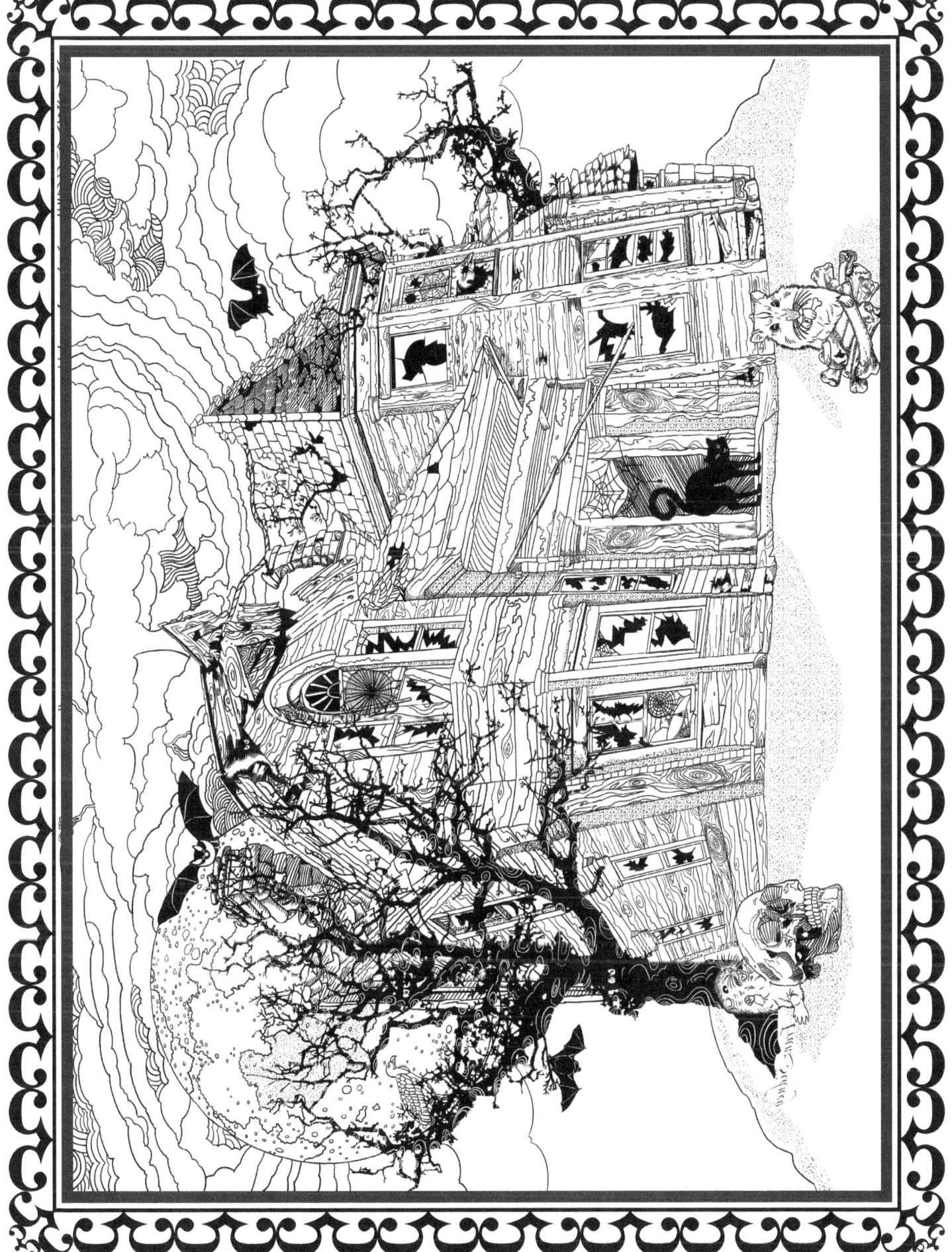

"IF PEOPLE KNEW HOW HARD I HAD TO WORK
TO GAIN MY MASTERY, IT WOULD NOT SEEM
SO WONDERFUL AT ALL."
MICHELANGELO BUONARROTI

_____
_____
_____
_____
_____
_____
_____
_____
_____
_____
_____
_____
_____
_____
_____
_____

An advanced alien civilisation visits the model chosen by
Michelangelo for the statue of David. He and his lady-friend hold their
mobile phones, take a selfie and say............?
Caption the image on the right

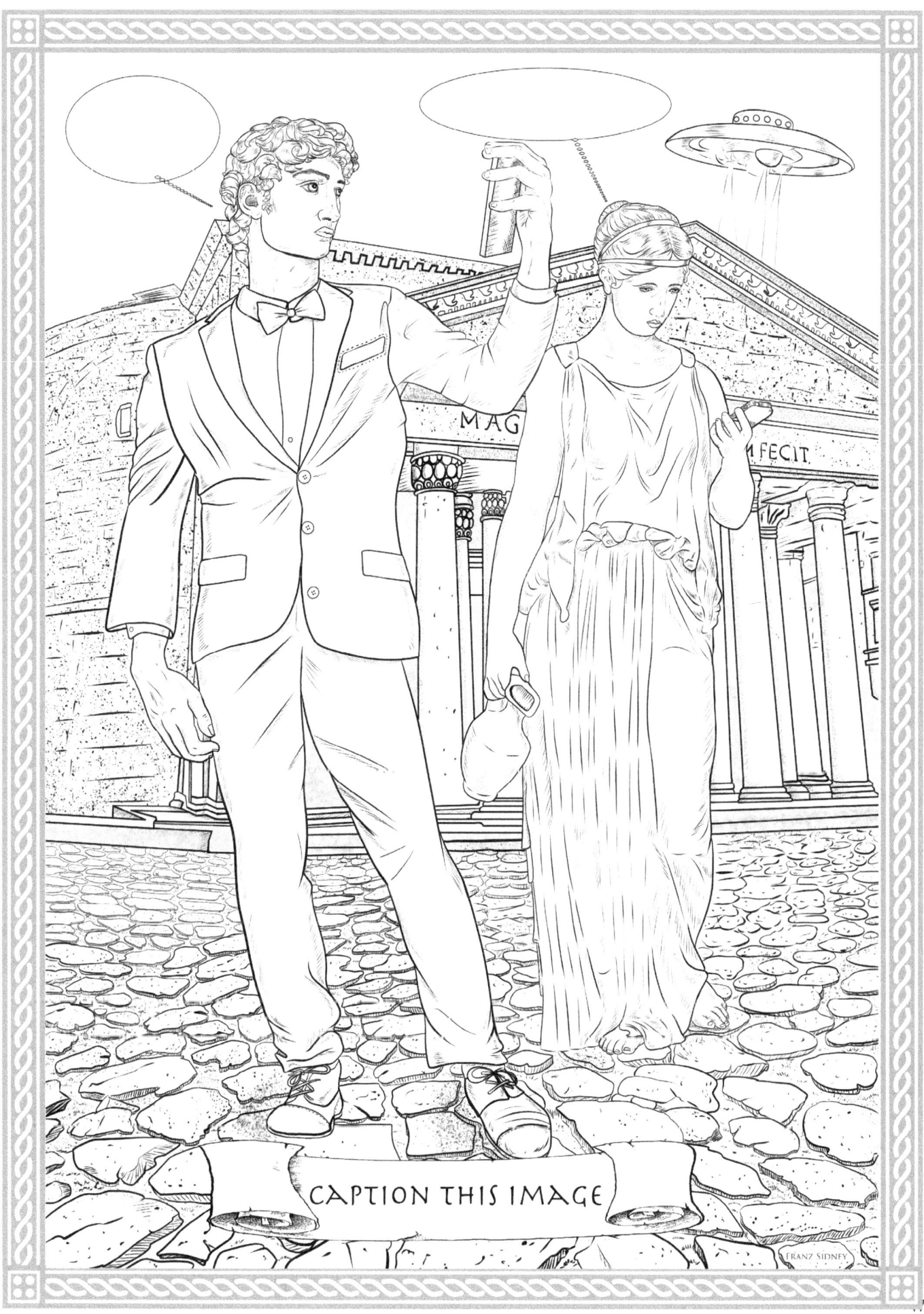

"IF YOU JUDGE PEOPLE, YOU HAVE
NO TIME TO LOVE THEM."
MOTHER TERESA

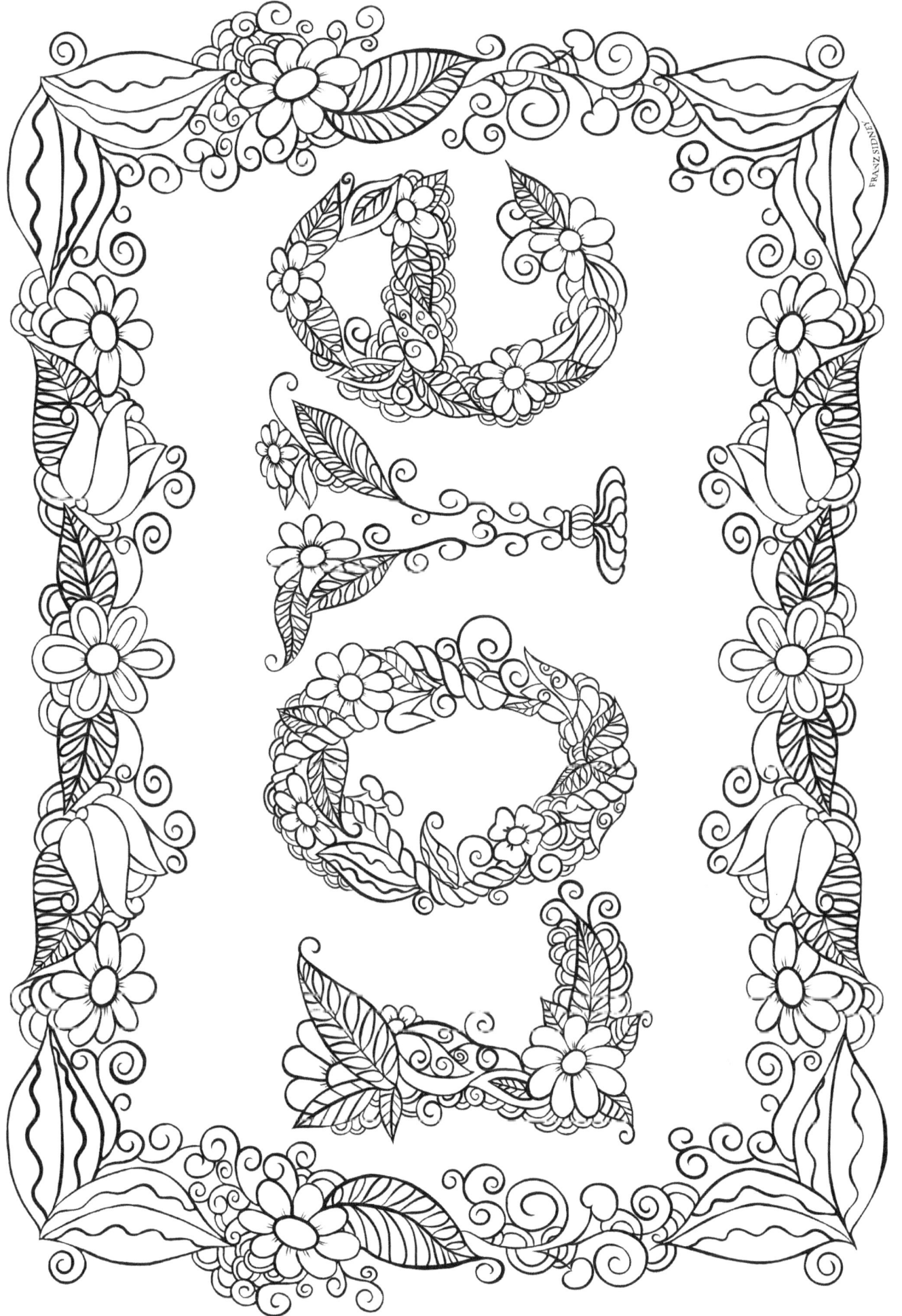

"BLUNDERS, NO, ONLY FRIENDSHIP BINDS US TO
HONESTY - ATTRACTING CRYPTS OF MUSHROOMS IN
THE WAKE OF OUR SNOWBOARDS."
BRADLEY CHICHO

_____
_____
_____
_____
_____
_____
_____
_____
_____
_____
_____
_____
_____
_____
_____
_____
_____
_____
_____
_____
_____

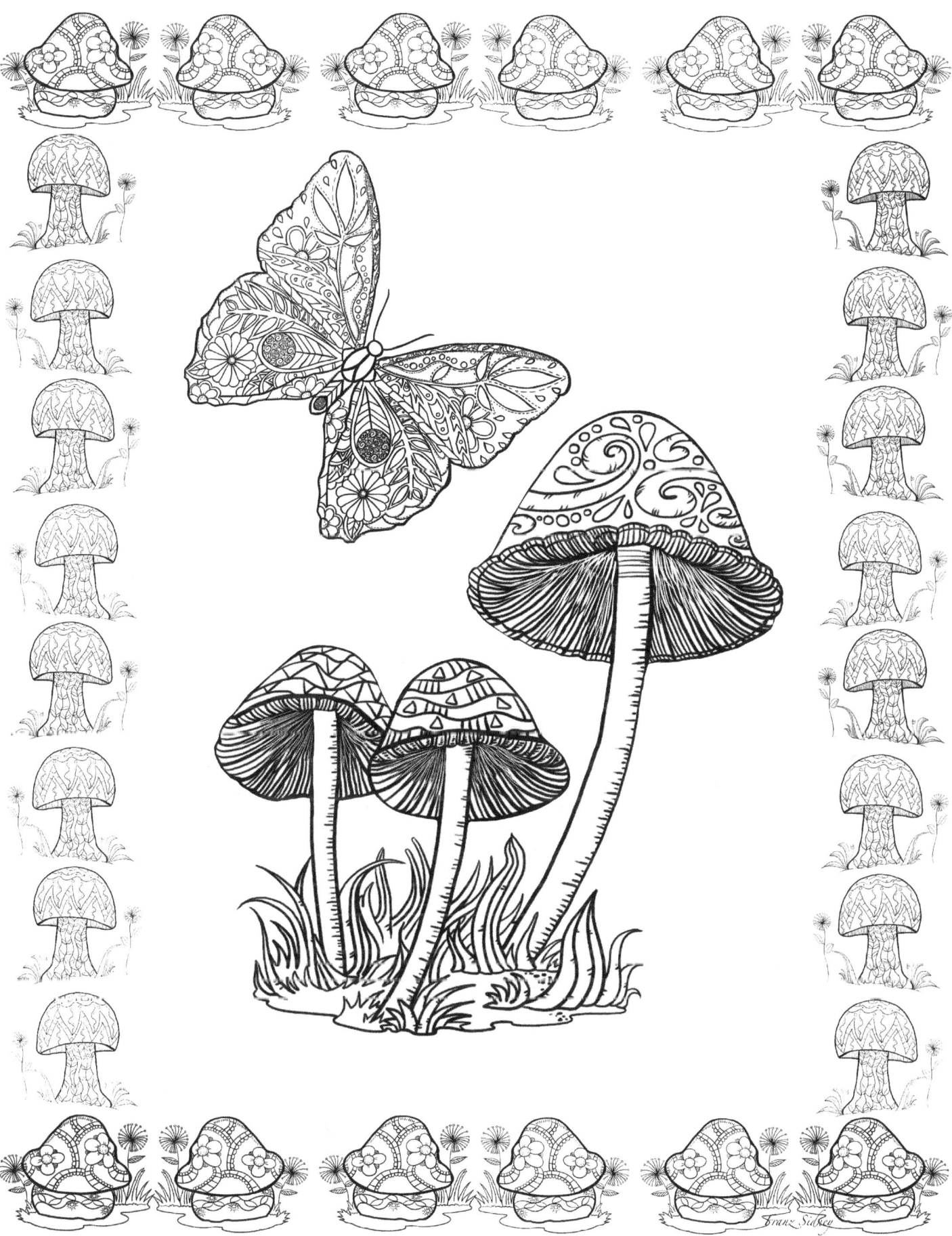

"THE SMALLEST FELINE IS A MASTERPIECE."
LEONARDO DA VINCI

_____

_____

_____

_____

_____

_____

_____

_____

_____

_____

_____

_____

_____

_____

_____

_____

_____

_____

_____

_____

_____

_____

_____

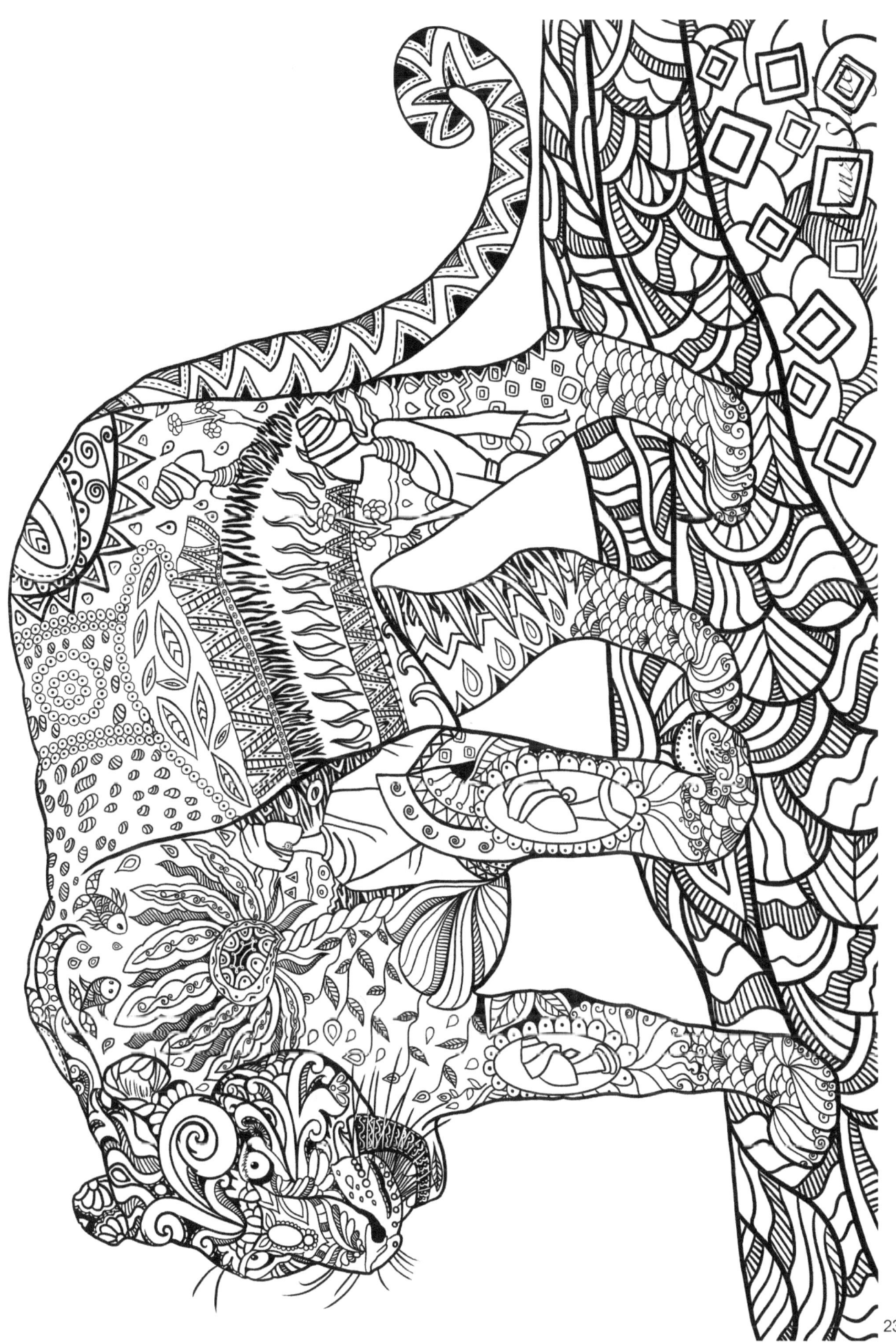

HOʻOPONOPONO

What is Hoʻoponopono?

Hoʻoponopono is an ancient Hawaiian practice used by families to achieve reconciliation and forgiveness.

It's a type of mental cleansing: the family gets together and goes through the four steps below to correct and restore good relationships among themselves and their God.

Family members say these words to one another. There are plenty of books and online resources if you want to learn more about this practice.

However, it's simple to practice Hoʻoponopono in four steps:

Step 1: Repentance – I'M SORRY
Step 2: Ask Forgiveness – PLEASE FORGIVE ME
Step 3: Gratitude – THANK YOU
Step 4: Love – I LOVE YOU

The world needs Hoʻoponopono!

_____
_____
_____
_____
_____
_____
_____
_____
_____
_____
_____
_____
_____
_____

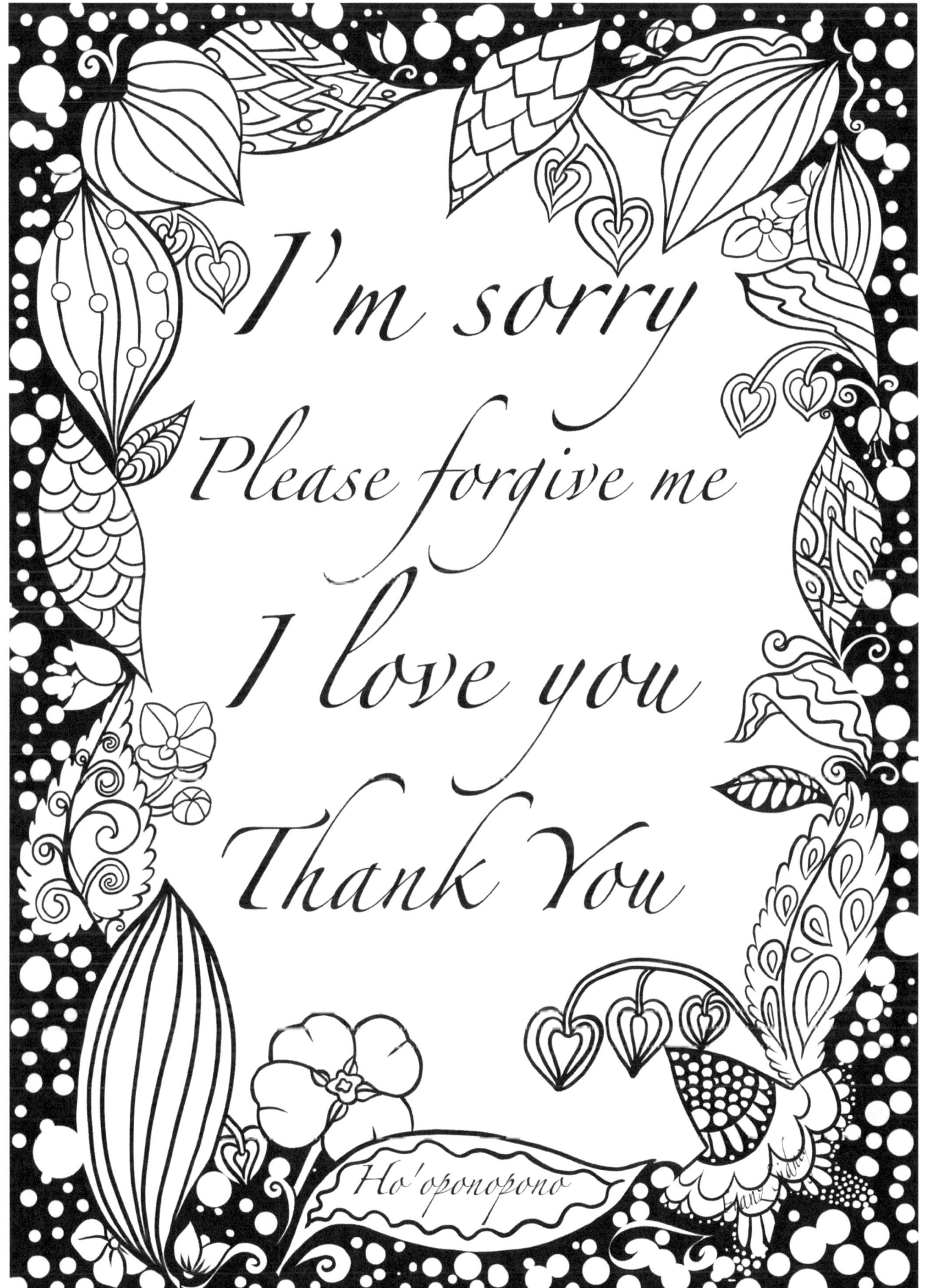

I'm sorry
Please forgive me
I love you
Thank You

Ho'oponopono

"HOW COULD ONE BE IN THIS WORLD WITHOUT
FEELING DISMAYED BY IT? EVEN IF ONE PAINTS
FLOWERS AND GINGERBREAD."
GERHARD RICHTER

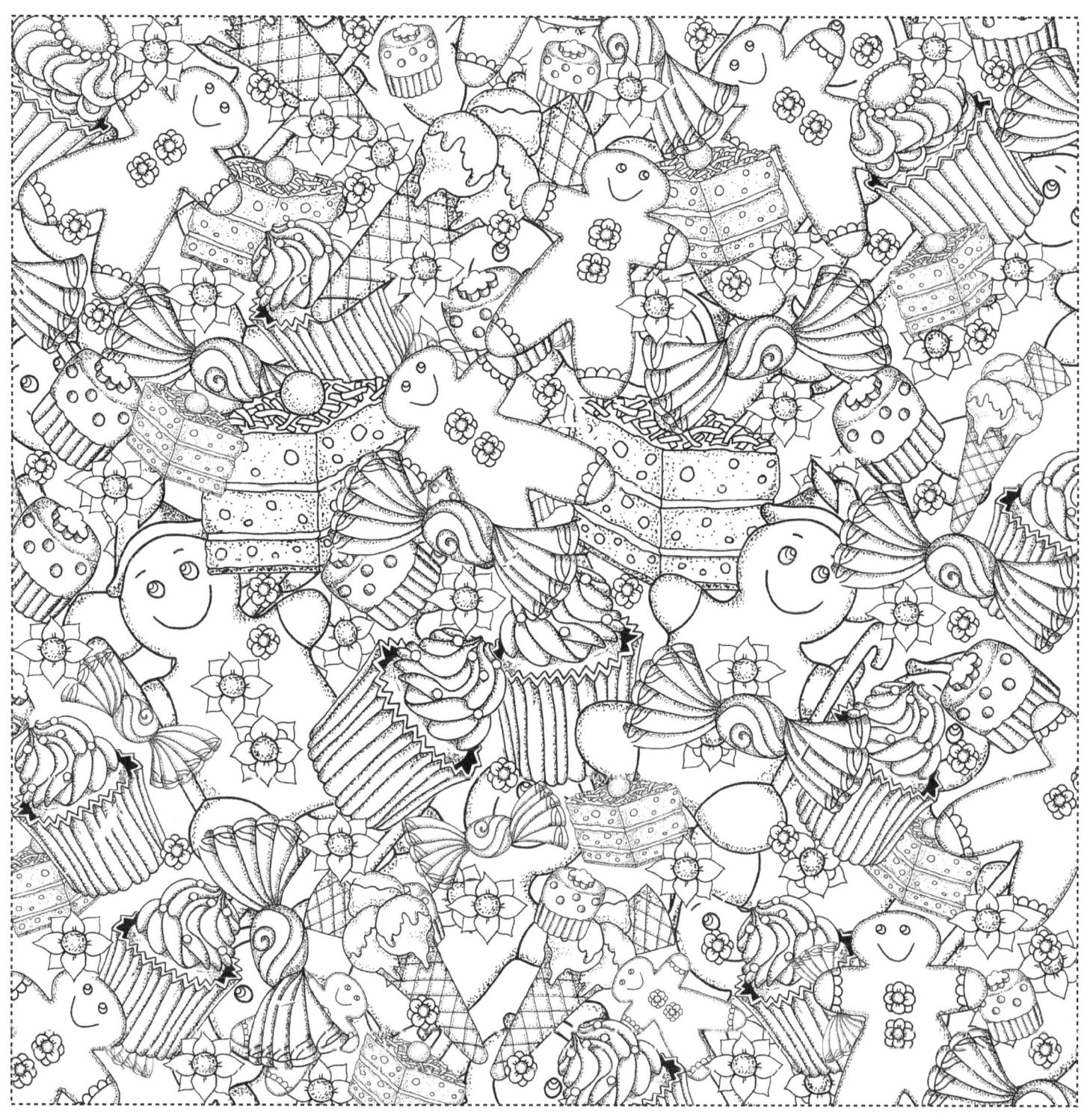

> "FOR WHATEVER WE LOSE (LIKE A YOU OR A ME),
> IT'S ALWAYS OUR SELF WE FIND IN THE SEA."
> E.E. CUMMINGS

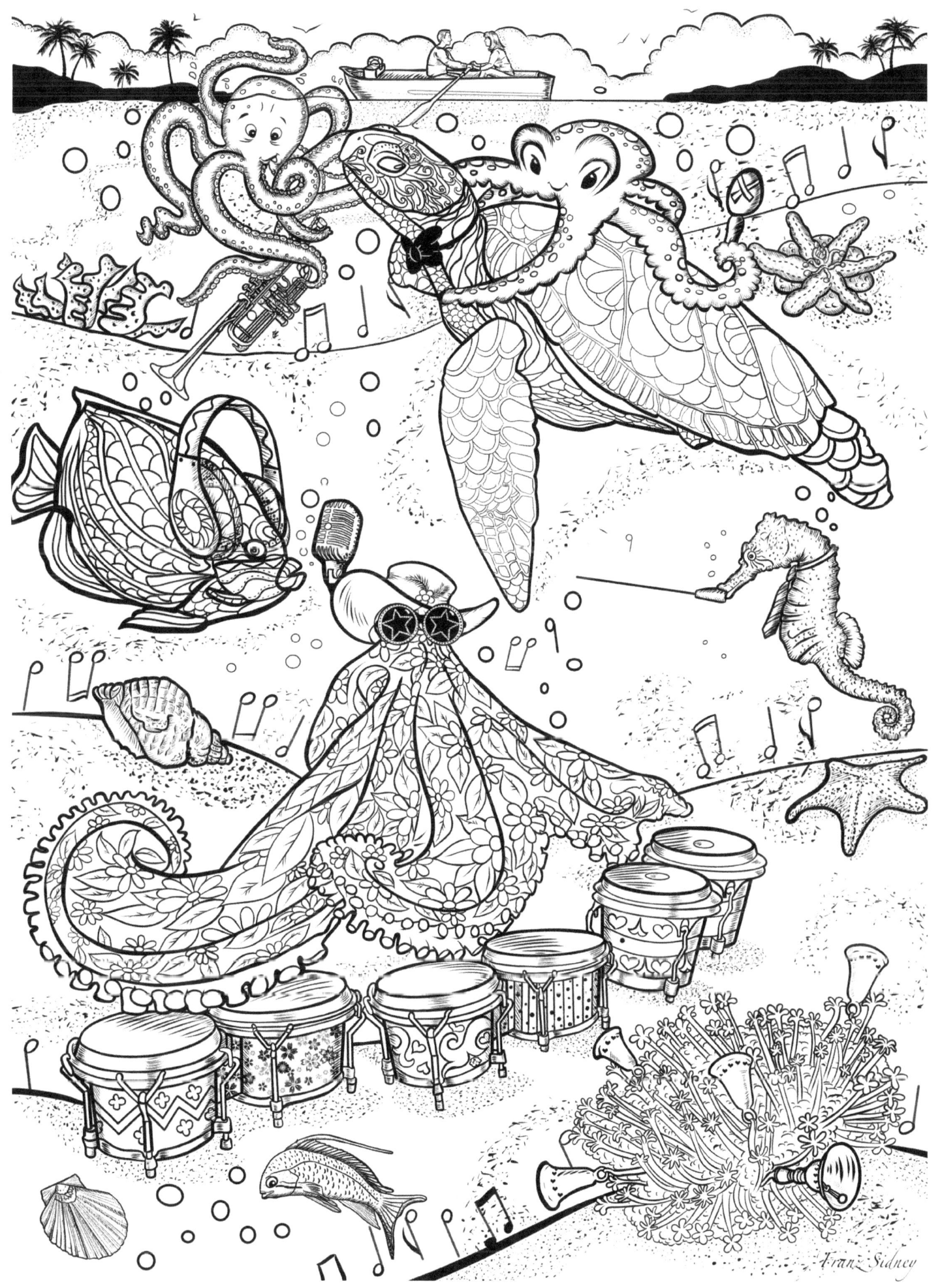

"A MOTHER'S ARMS ARE MADE OF TENDERNESS AND
CHILDREN SLEEP SOUNDLY IN THEM."
VICTOR HUGO

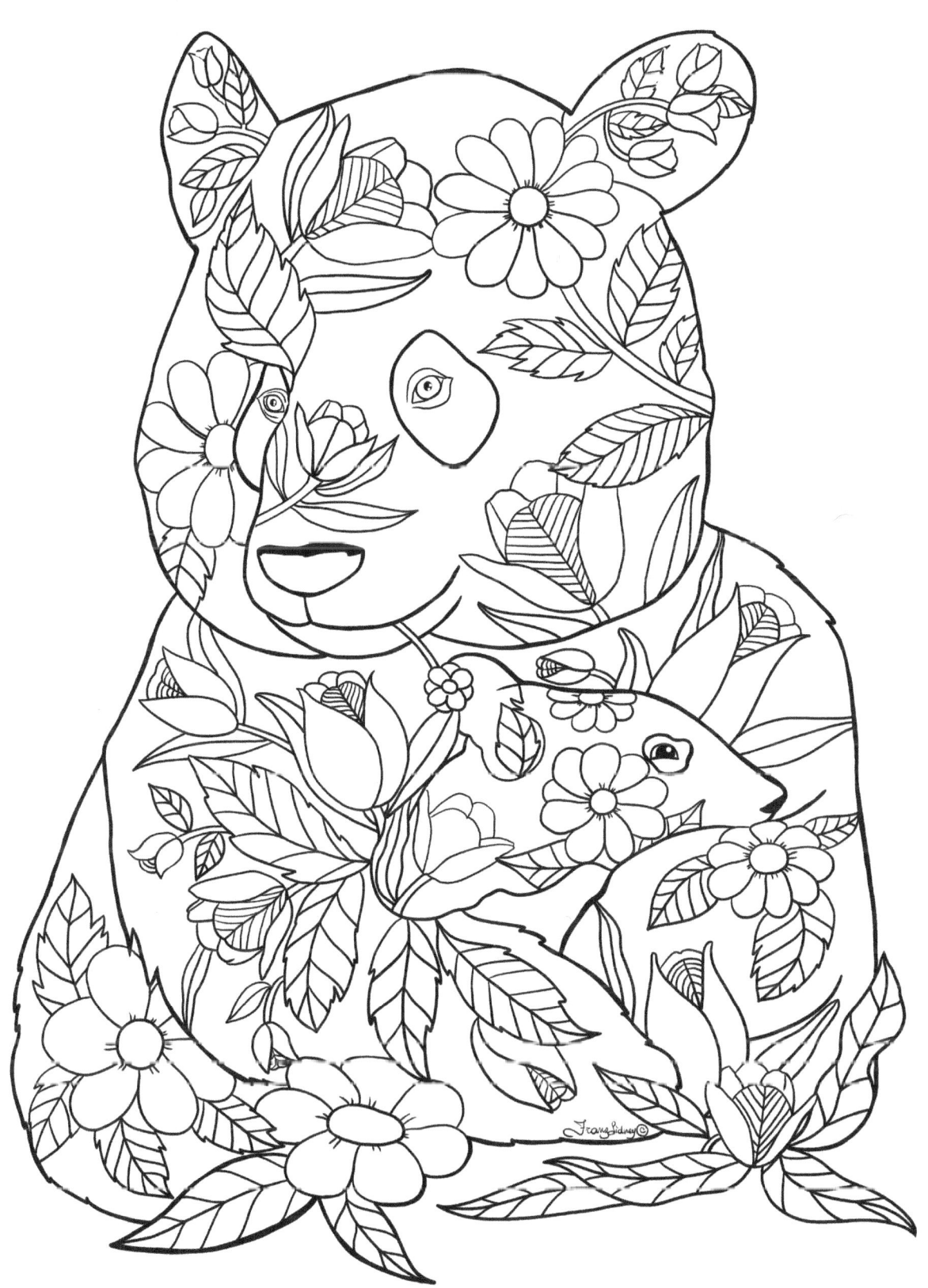

> "SWORDS CAN WIN TERRITORIES BUT NOT HEARTS,
> FORCES CAN BEND HEADS BUT NOT MINDS."
> MIRZA TAHIR AHMAD

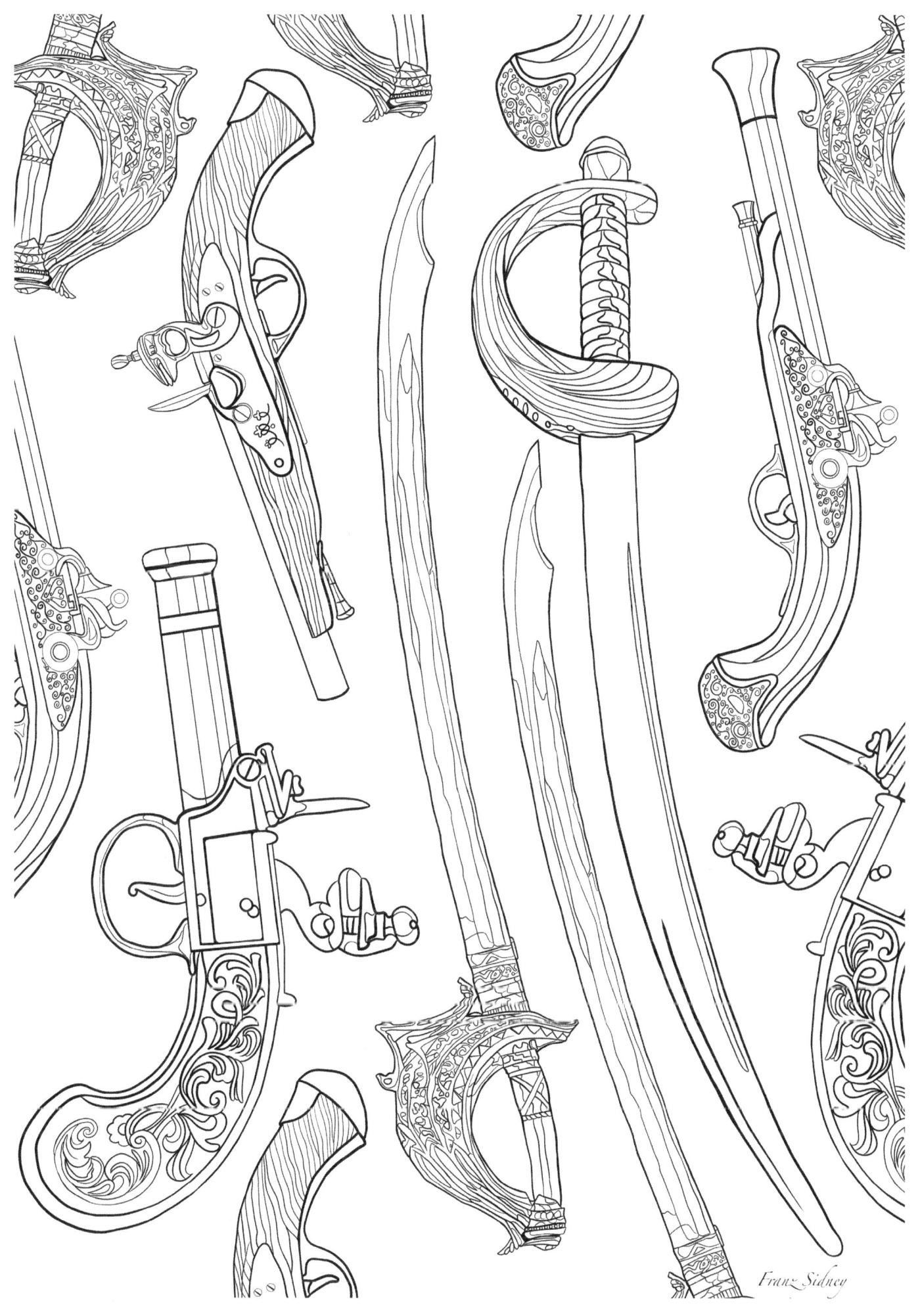

Franz Sidney

"ALL YOU NEED IS THE PLAN, THE ROAD MAP, AND THE
COURAGE TO PRESS ON TO YOUR DESTINATION."
EARL NIGHTINGALE

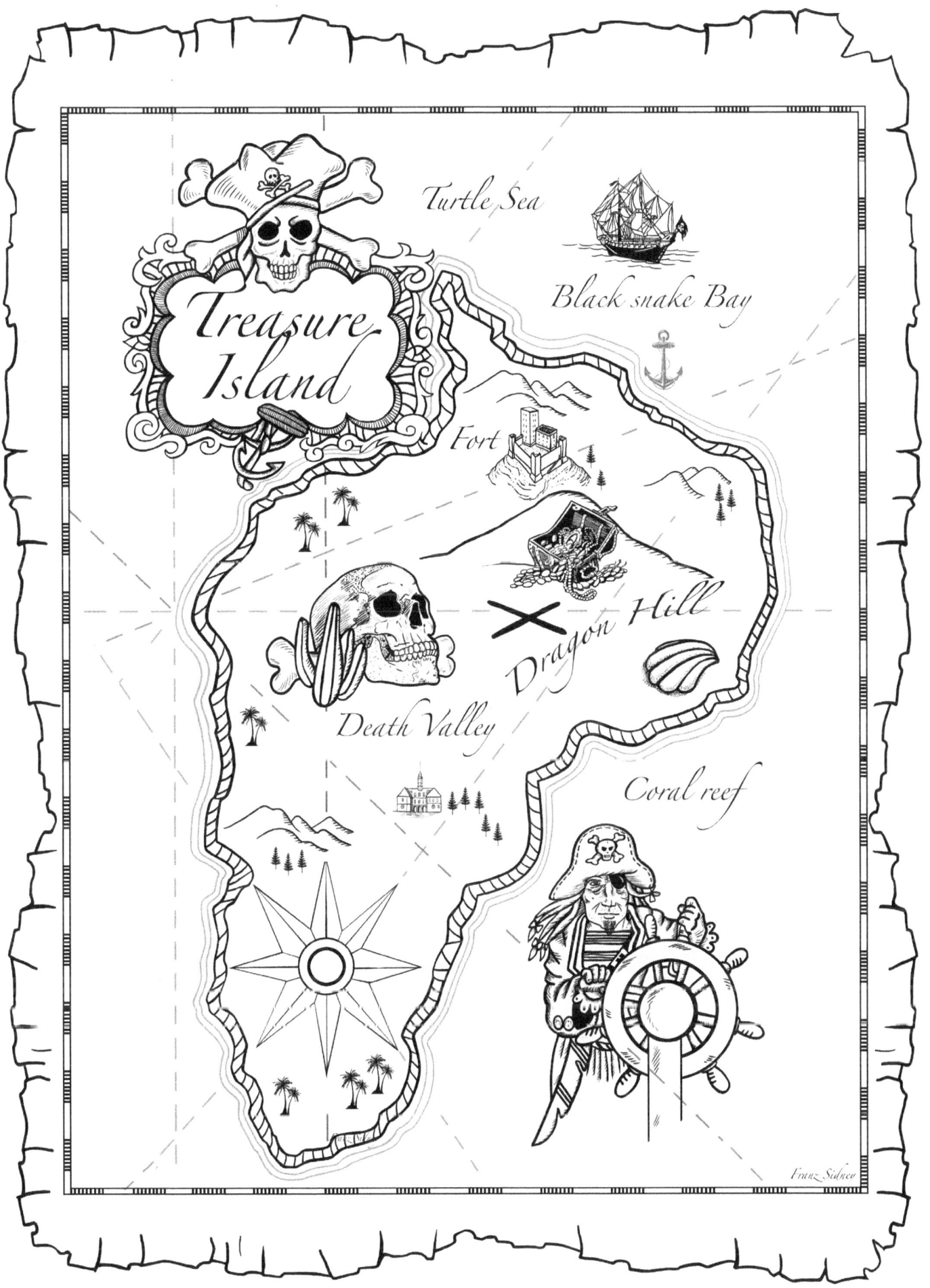

"THE SEA, ONCE IT CASTS ITS SPELL, HOLDS ONE
IN ITS NET OF WONDER FOREVER."
JACQUES YVES COUSTEAU

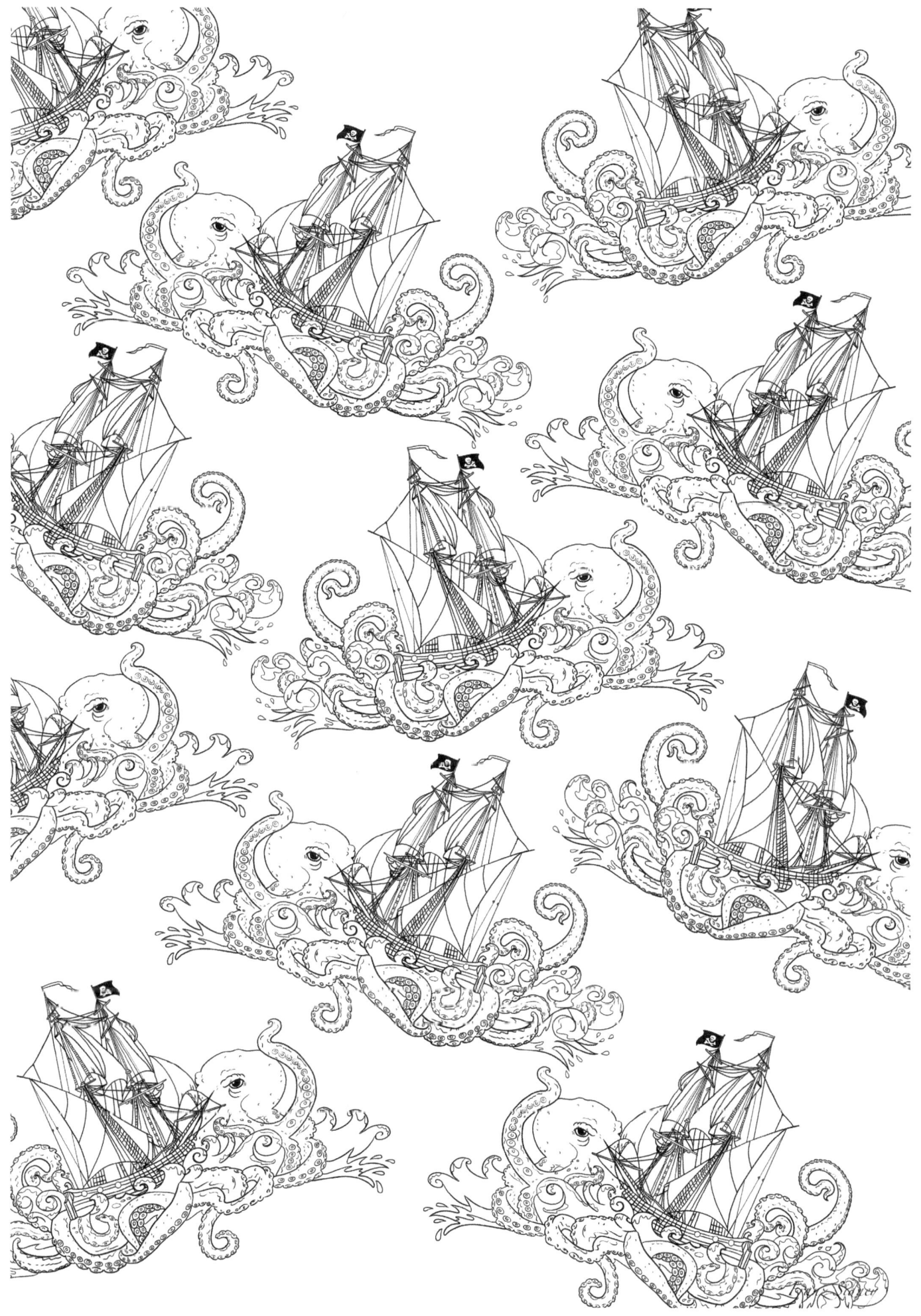

"A HORSE IS THE PROJECTION OF PEOPLES' DREAMS
ABOUT THEMSELVES - STRONG, POWERFUL, BEAUTIFUL -
AND IT HAS THE CAPABILITY OF GIVING US ESCAPE
FROM OUR MUNDANE EXISTENCE."
PAM BROWN

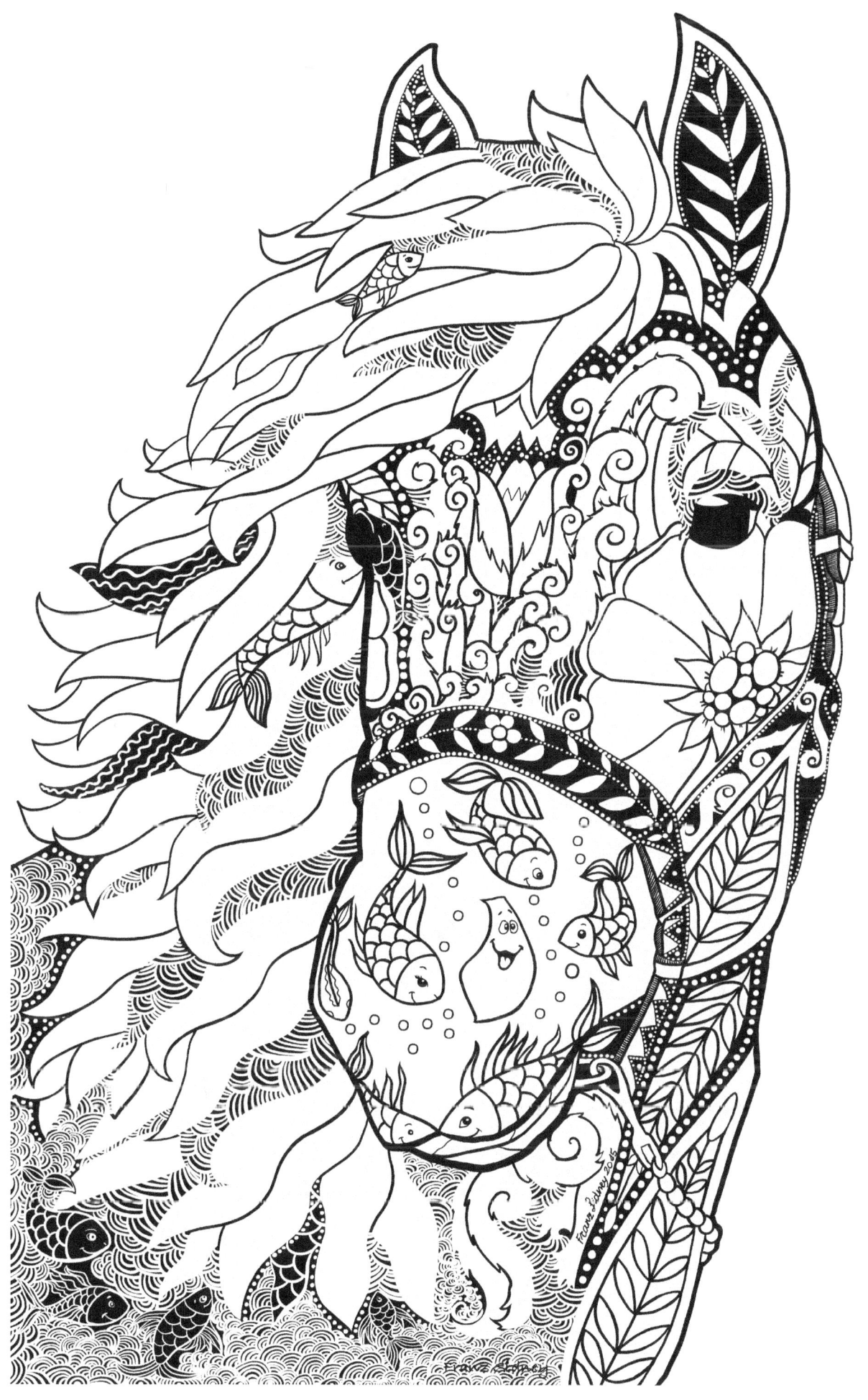

"HOW MANY OBSERVE CHRIST'S BIRTHDAY! HOW FEW, HIS PRECEPTS!"
BENJAMIN FRANKLIN

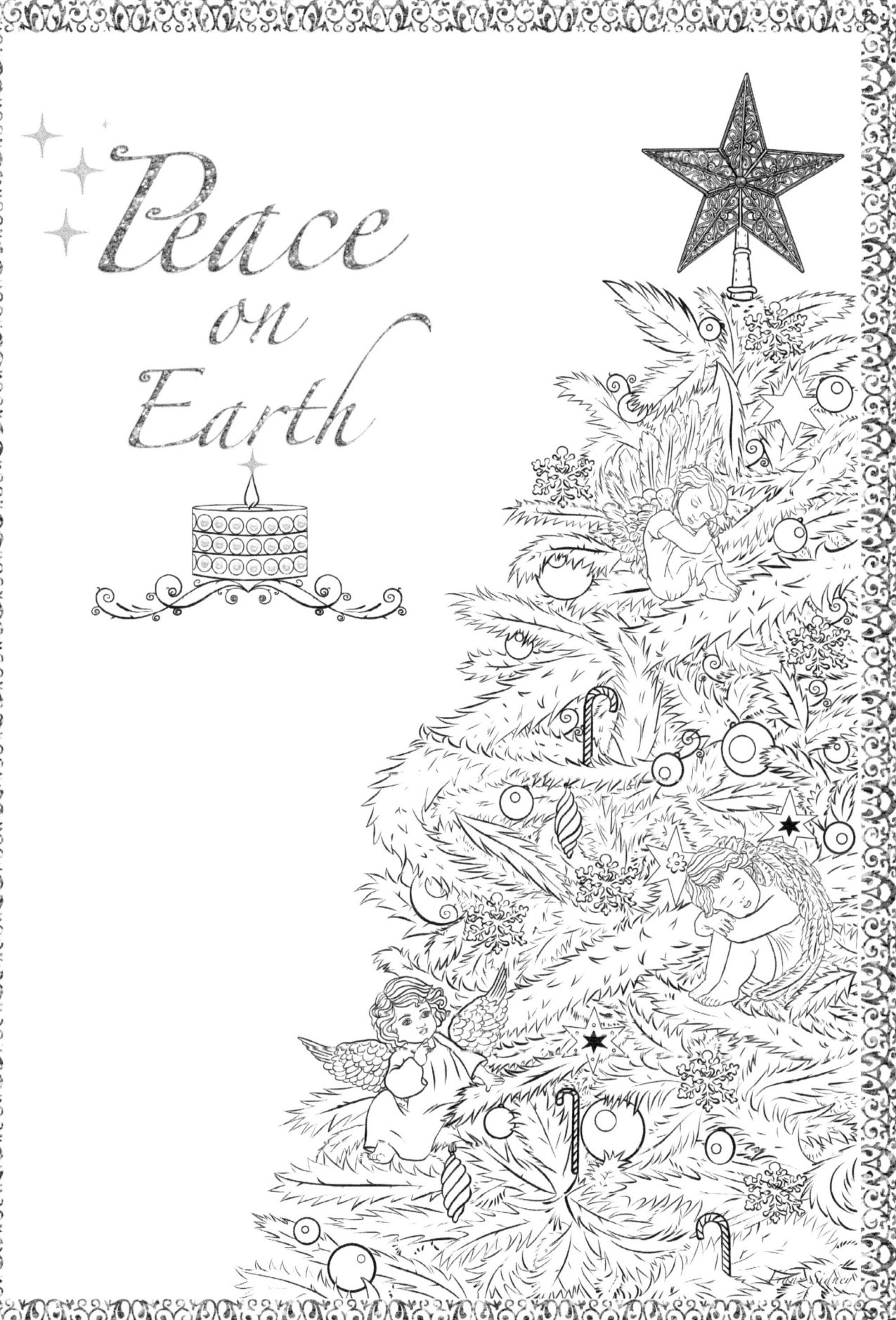

Peace on Earth

"IF THE SKY COULD DREAM,
IT WOULD DREAM OF DRAGONS."
LLONA ANDREWS, FATE'S EDGE

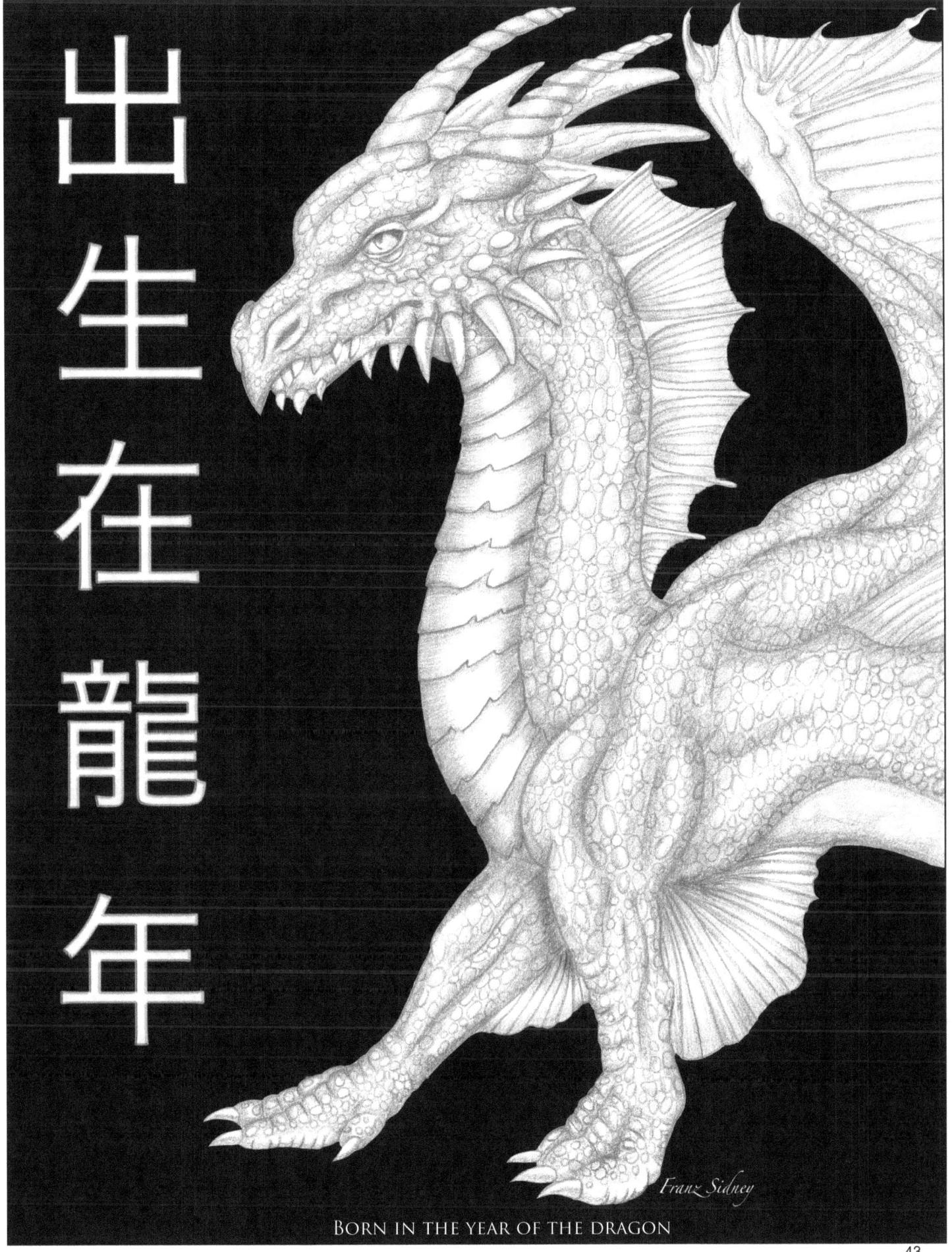

出生在龍年

Franz Sidney

BORN IN THE YEAR OF THE DRAGON

"IF YOUR MOM ASKS YOU TO DO THE DISHES, DO NOT PULL OUT YOUR PIRATE ATTITUDE. BUT IF SOMEONE TELLS YOU YOU'RE NOT GOOD ENOUGH, SAYS YOUR DREAMS ARE TOO LOFTY, OR CLAIMS THERE IS NO ROOM IN SHOWBIZ FOR A DANCING VIOLINIST - WELL THEN, BY ALL MEANS, PULL OUT YOUR EYE PATCH, MY FRIEND, AND TAKE TO THE HIGH SEAS."
LINDSEY STIRLING

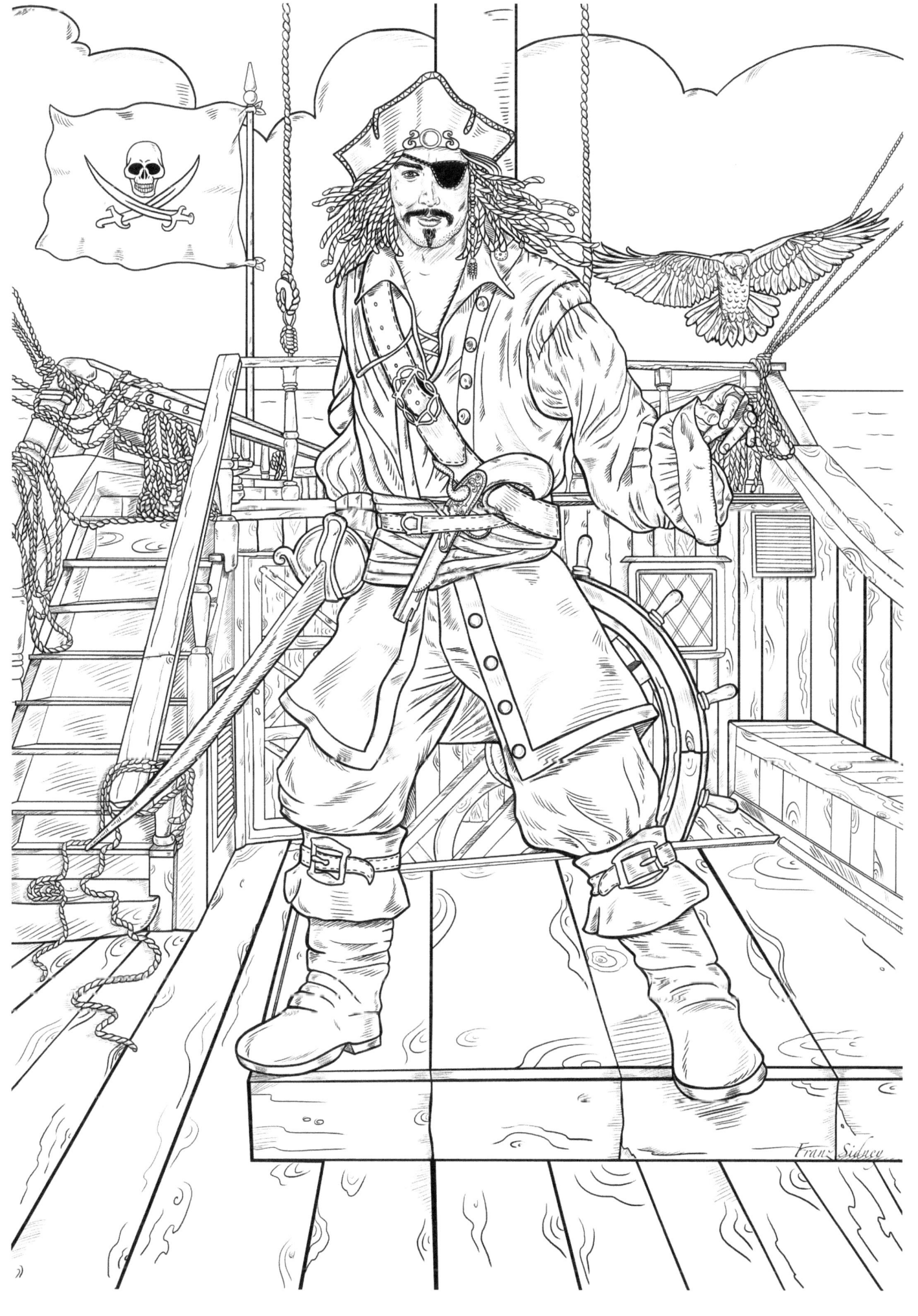

Franz Sidney

"THERE ARE THREE FAITHFUL FRIENDS - AN OLD WIFE, AN OLD DOG, AND READY MONEY."
BENJAMIN FRANKLIN

_____
_____
_____
_____
_____
_____
_____
_____
_____
_____
_____
_____
_____
_____
_____
_____
_____
_____
_____
_____
_____
_____
_____

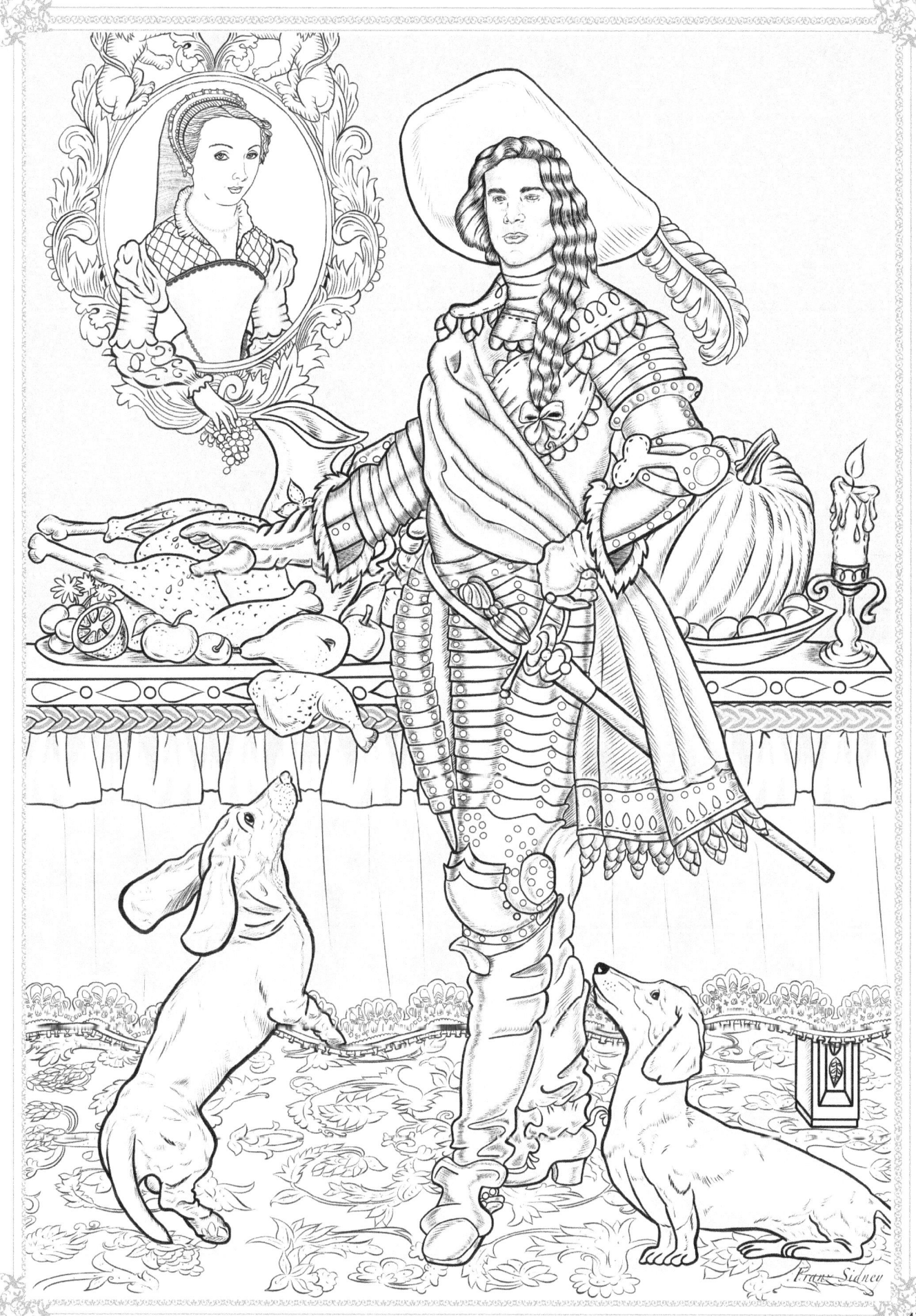

Franz Sidney

"LIVE IN SUCH A WAY THAT YOU WOULD NOT BE
ASHAMED TO SELL YOUR PARROT
TO THE TOWN GOSSIP."
WILL ROGERS

_____
_____
_____
_____
_____
_____
_____
_____
_____
_____
_____
_____
_____
_____
_____
_____
_____
_____
_____
_____
_____
_____
_____

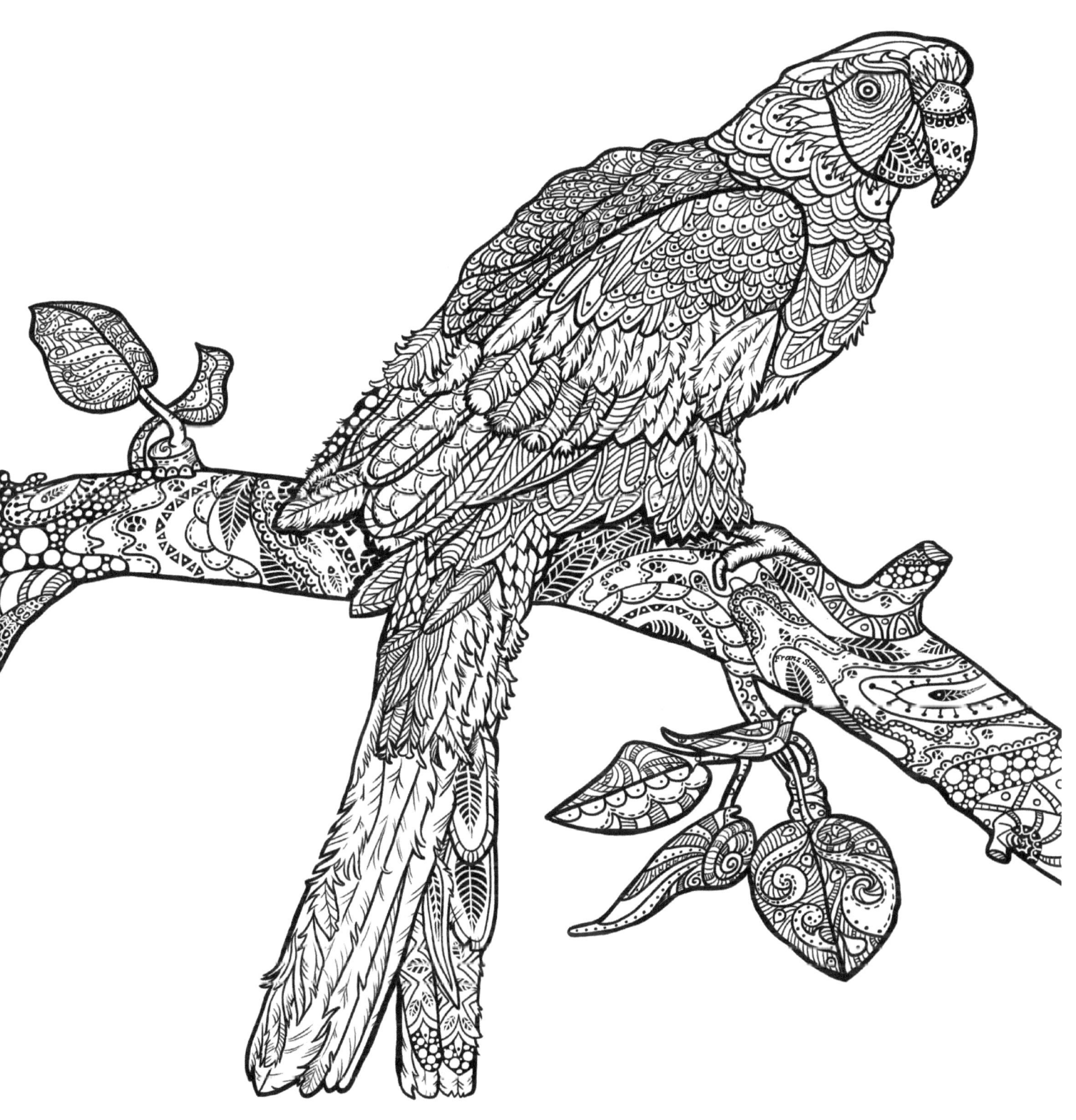

"IF SOMEONE THINKS THAT PEACE AND LOVE ARE JUST A CLICHE THAT MUST HAVE BEEN LEFT BEHIND IN THE 60S, THAT'S A PROBLEM. PEACE AND LOVE ARE ETERNAL."
JOHN LENNON

_____

_____

_____

_____

_____

_____

_____

_____

_____

_____

_____

_____

_____

_____

_____

_____

_____

_____

_____

_____

_____

_____

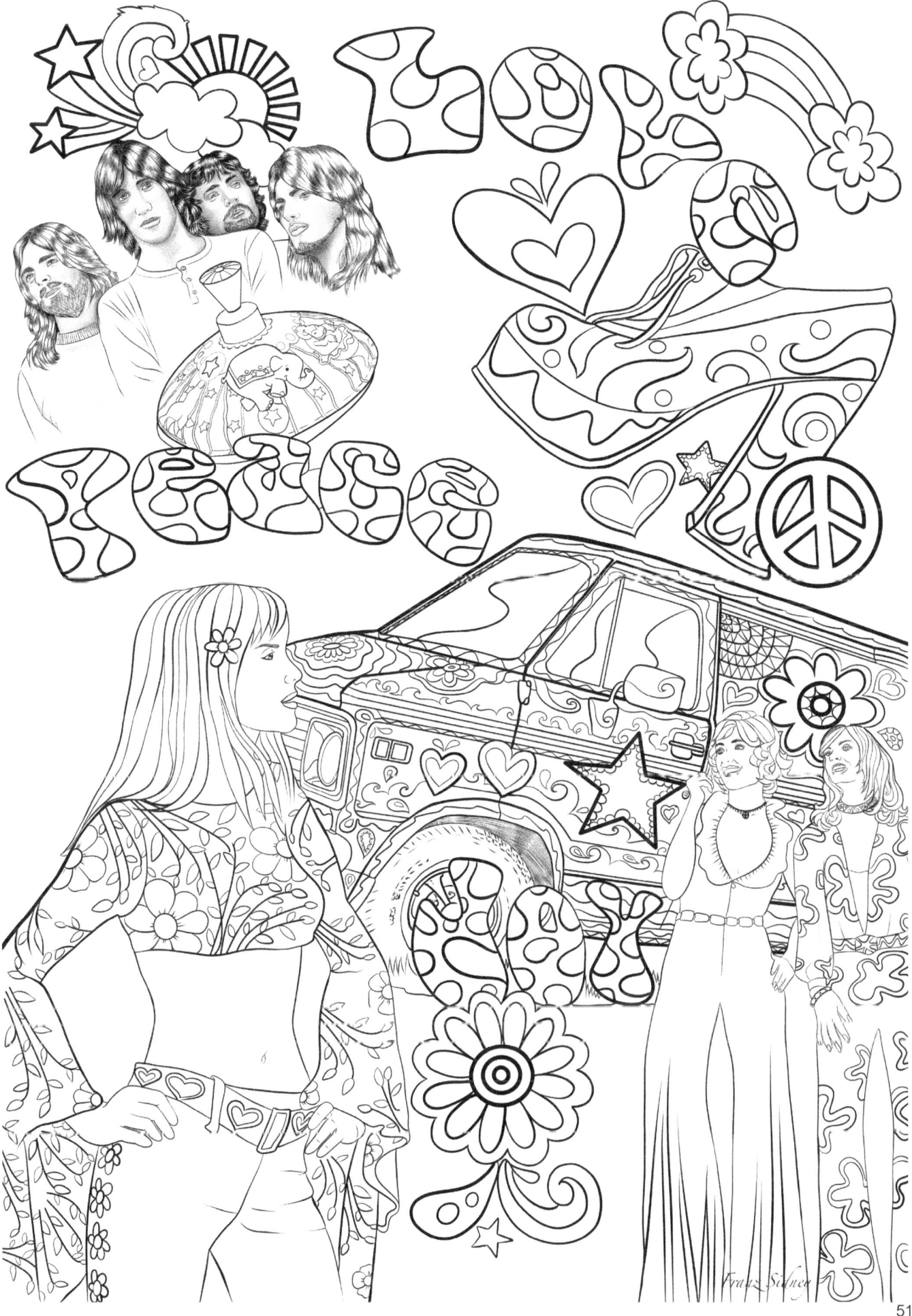

"CHILDREN WILL NOT REMEMBER YOU FOR THE
MATERIAL THINGS YOU PROVIDED BUT FOR
THE FEELING THAT YOU CHERISHED THEM."
RICHARD L. EVANS

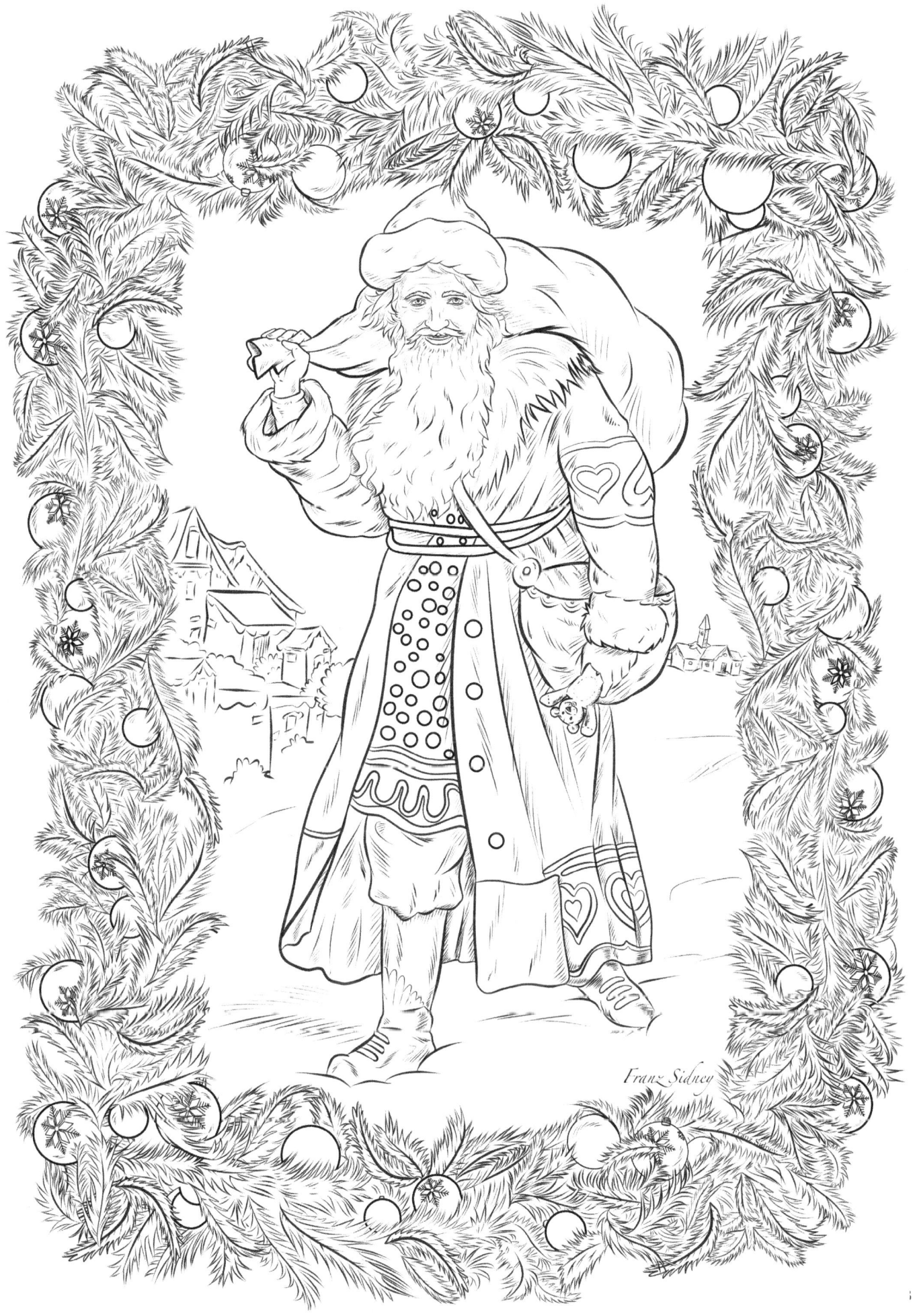

Franz Sidney

"THERE IS MORE TREASURE IN BOOKS THAN IN ALL THE PIRATES' LOOT ON TREASURE ISLAND AND BEST OF ALL, YOU CAN ENJOY THESE RICHES EVERY DAY OF YOUR LIFE."
WALT DISNEY COMPANY

_____

_____

_____

_____

_____

_____

_____

_____

_____

_____

_____

_____

_____

_____

_____

_____

_____

_____

_____

_____

_____

_____

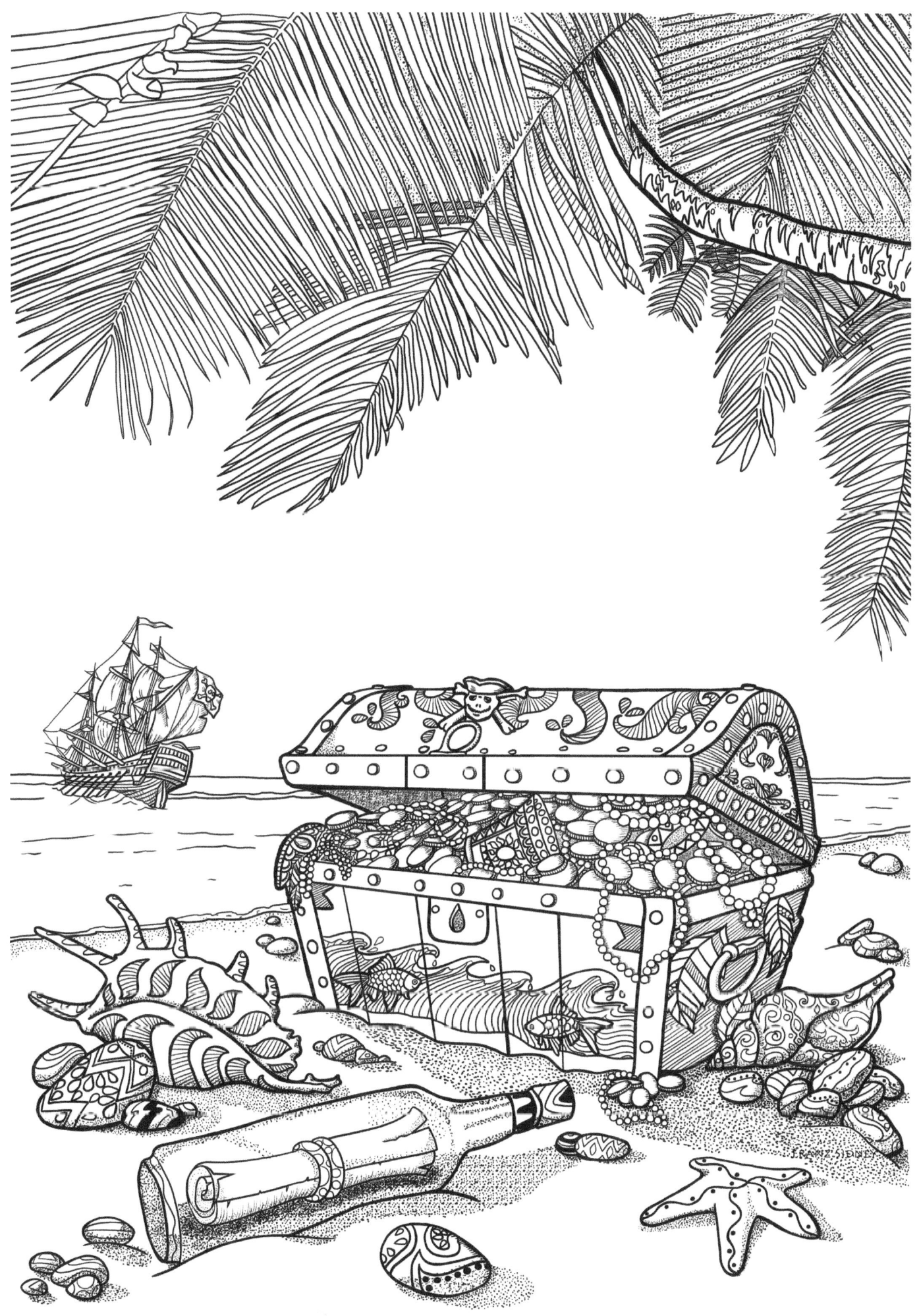

"IF I HAD A FLOWER FOR EVERY TIME I THOUGHT OF YOU...I COULD WALK THROUGH MY GARDEN FOREVER."
ALFRED TENNYSON

"THERE IS NO FRIEND AS LOYAL AS A BOOK."
ERNEST HEMINGWAY

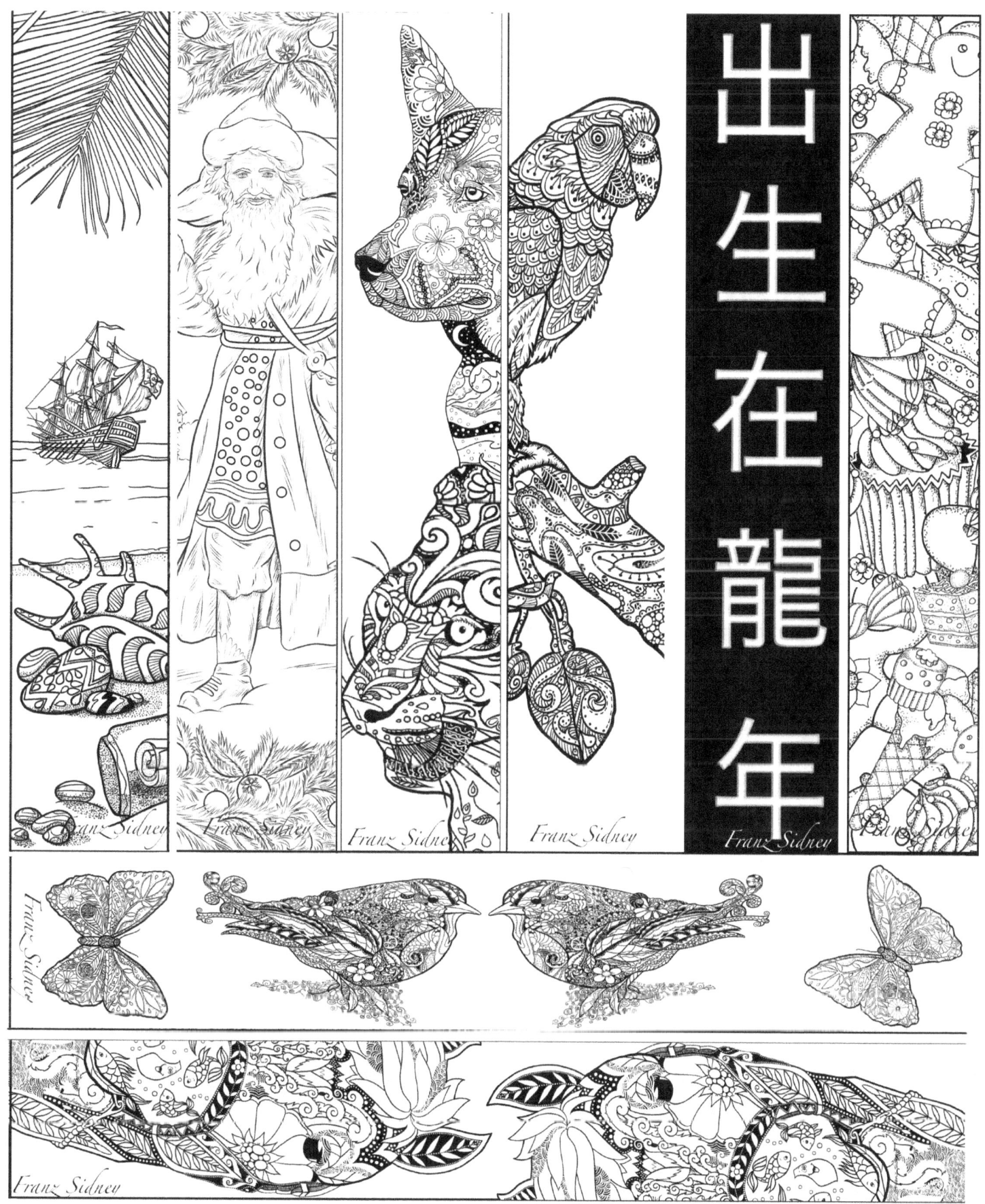

出生在龍年

Franz Sidney

Bookmarks

"FIND A PLACE INSIDE WHERE THERE'S JOY, AND THE JOY WILL BURN OUT THE PAIN."
JOSEPH CAMPBELL

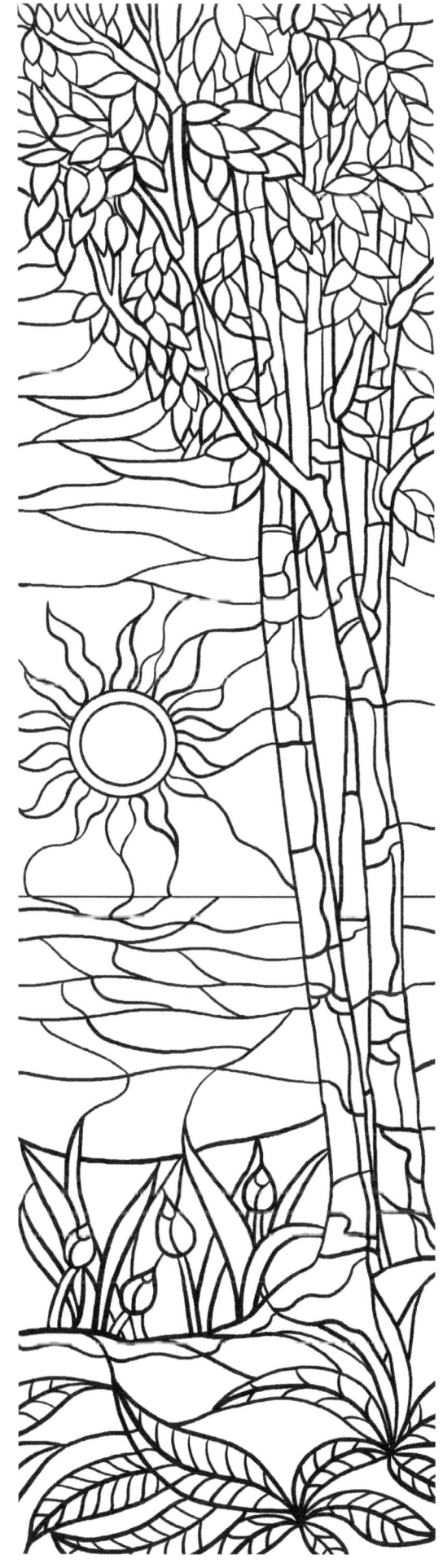

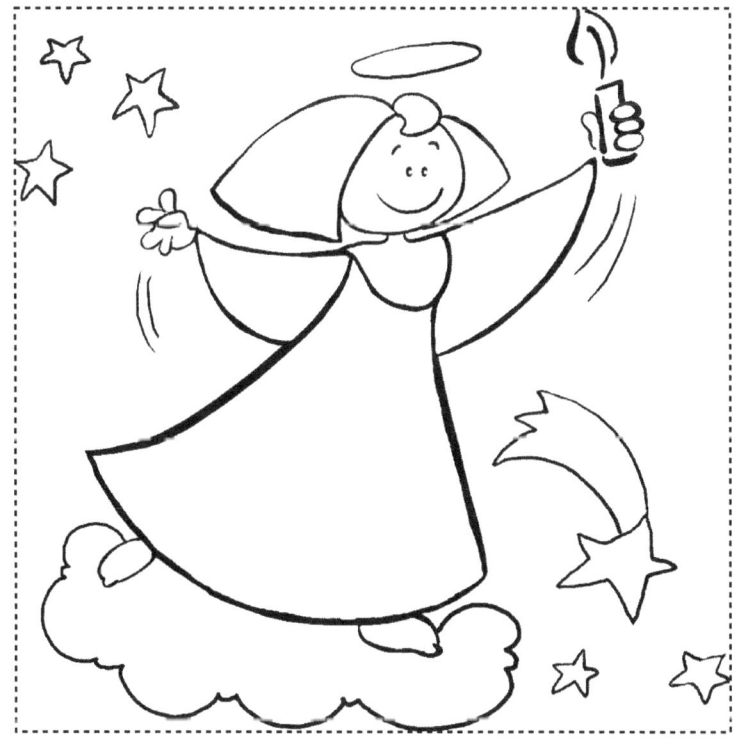

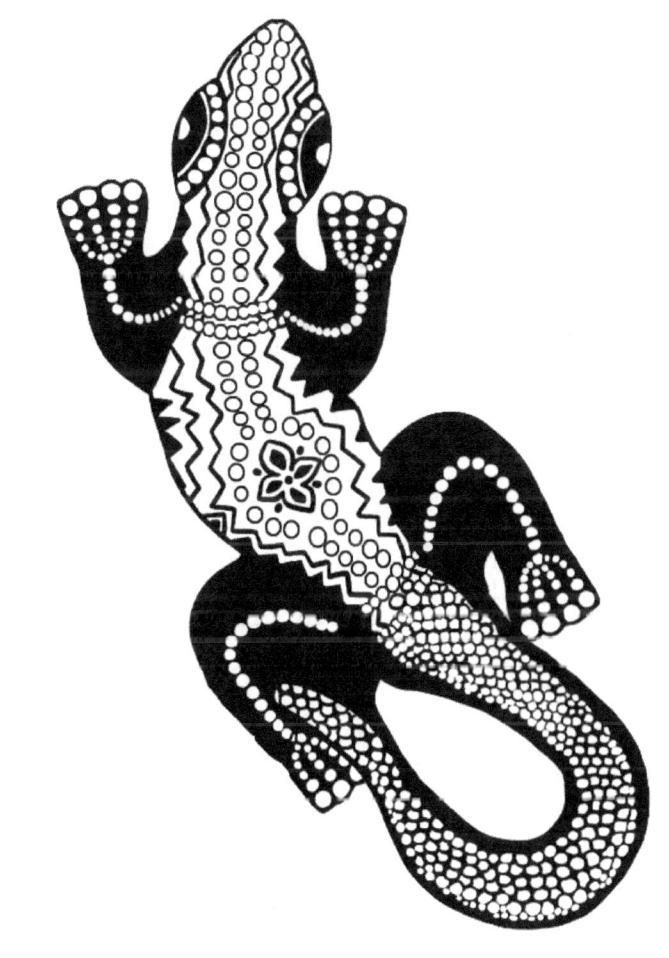

"THE WAILING OWL SCREAMS SOLITARY
TO THE MOURNFUL MOON."
DAVID MALLET

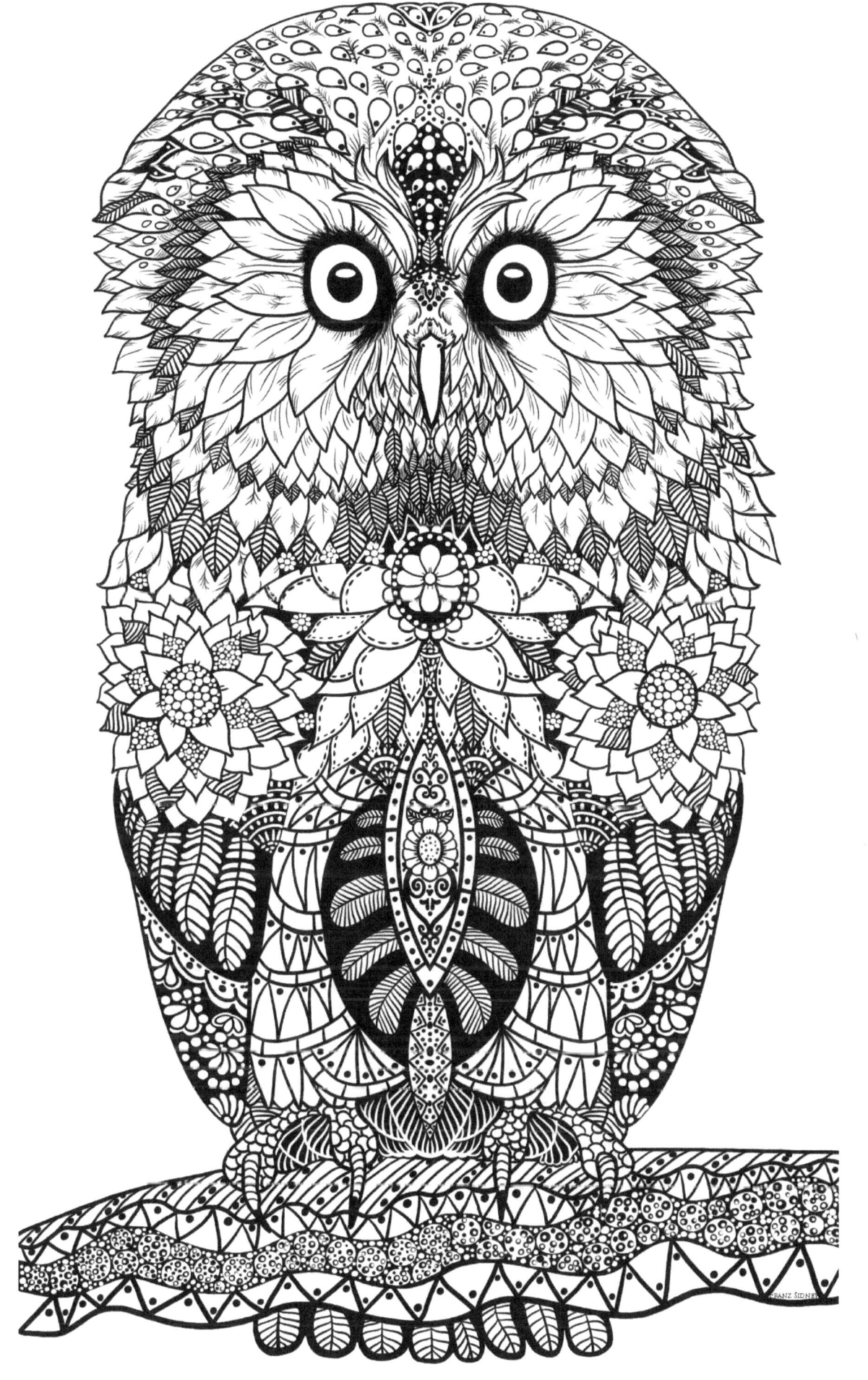

A "SNOW DAY LITERALLY AND FIGURATIVELY FALLS FROM
THE SKY, UNBIDDEN, AND SEEMS LIKE
A THING OF WONDER."
SUSAN ORLEAN

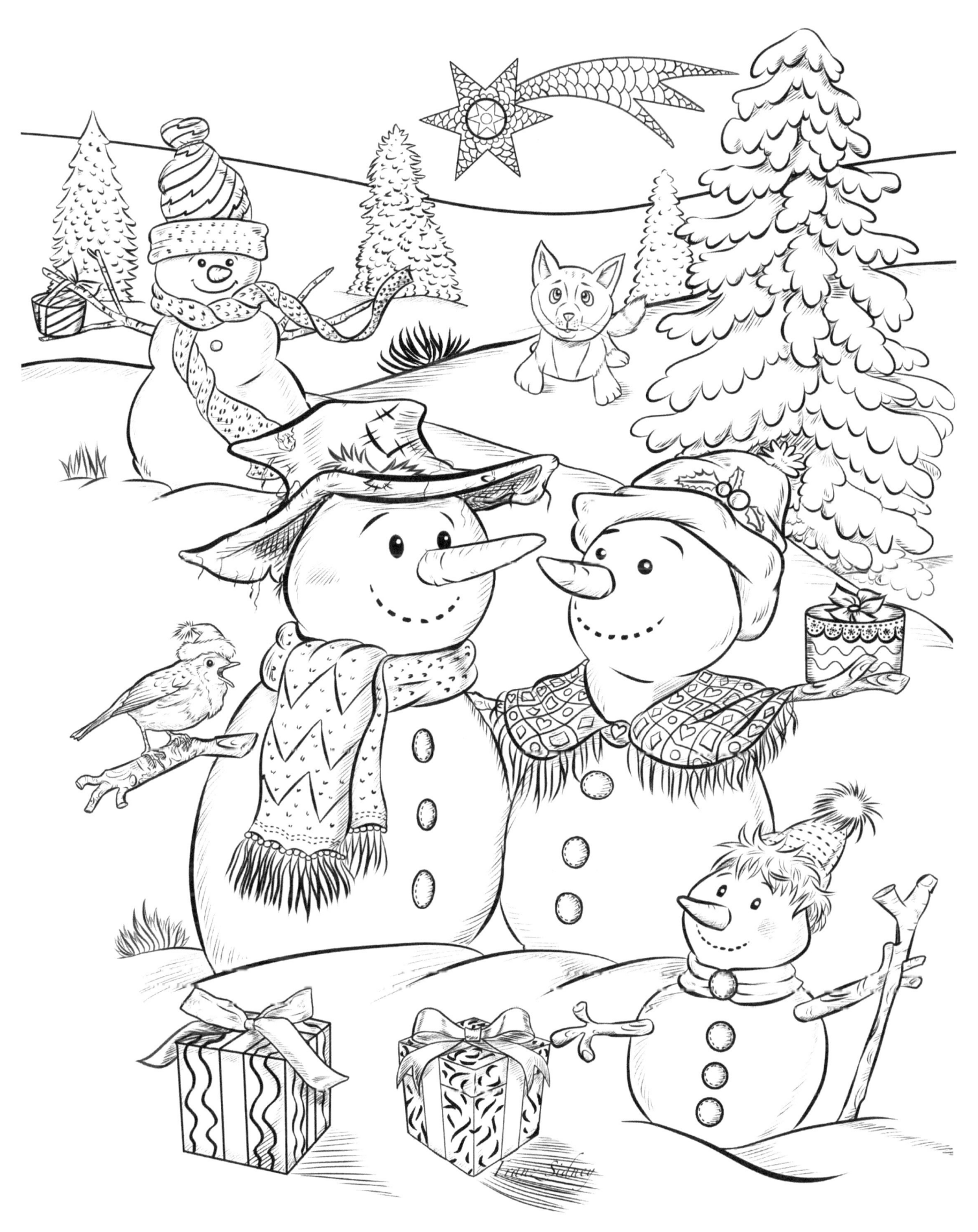

"HE WHO WOULD LEARN TO FLY ONE DAY MUST FIRST
LEARN TO STAND AND WALK AND RUN AND CLIMB AND
DANCE; ONE CANNOT FLY INTO FLYING."
FRIEDRICH NIETZSCHE

ANAX IMPERATOR (EMPEROR DRAGONFLY)

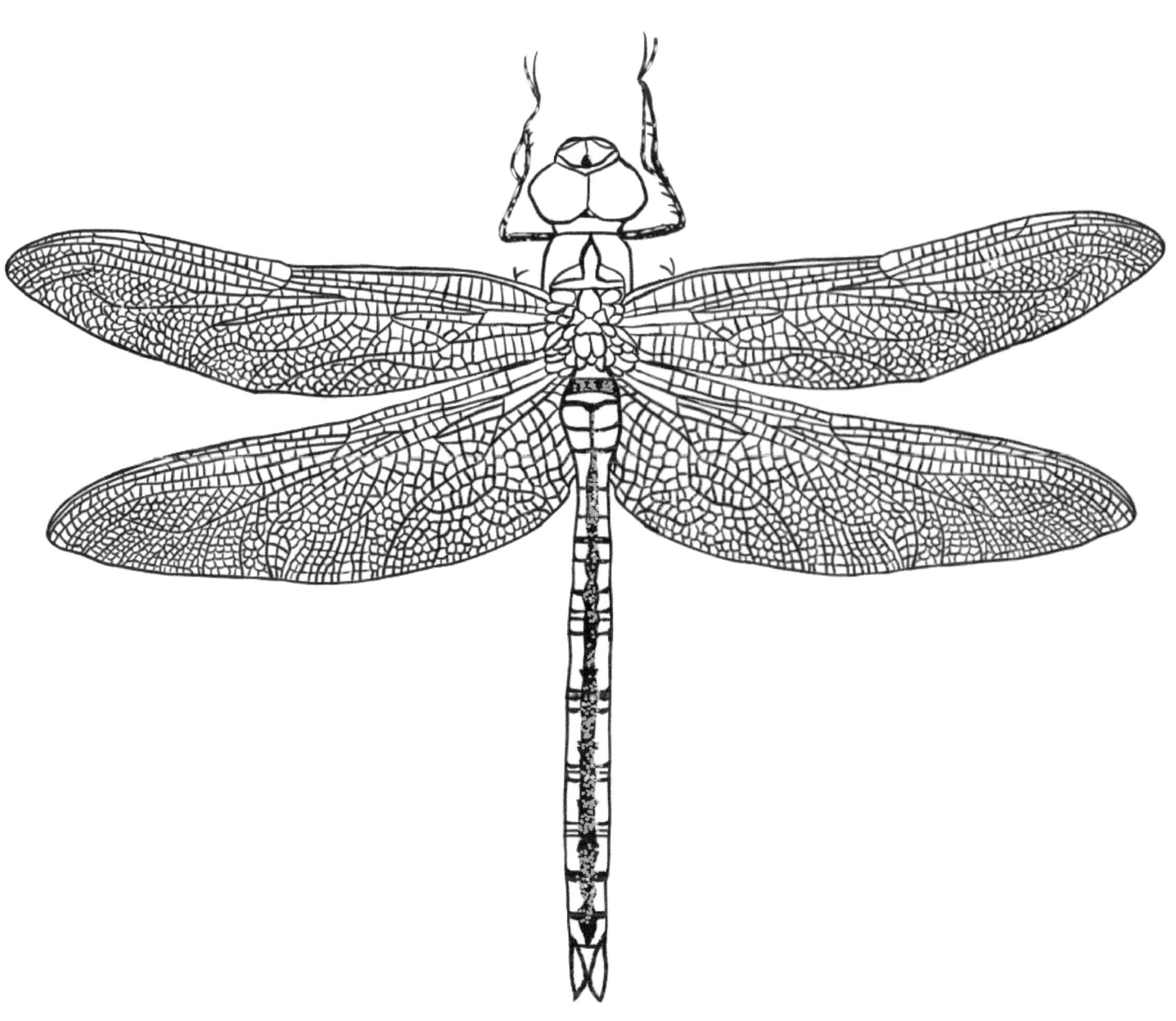

"THERE'S NOTHING WRONG WITH ENJOYING LOOKING AT THE SURFACE OF THE OCEAN ITSELF, EXCEPT THAT WHEN YOU FINALLY SEE WHAT GOES ON UNDERWATER, YOU REALIZE THAT YOU'VE BEEN MISSING THE WHOLE POINT OF THE OCEAN. STAYING ON THE SURFACE ALL THE TIME IS LIKE GOING TO THE CIRCUS AND STARING AT THE OUTSIDE OF THE TENT."
DAVE BARRY

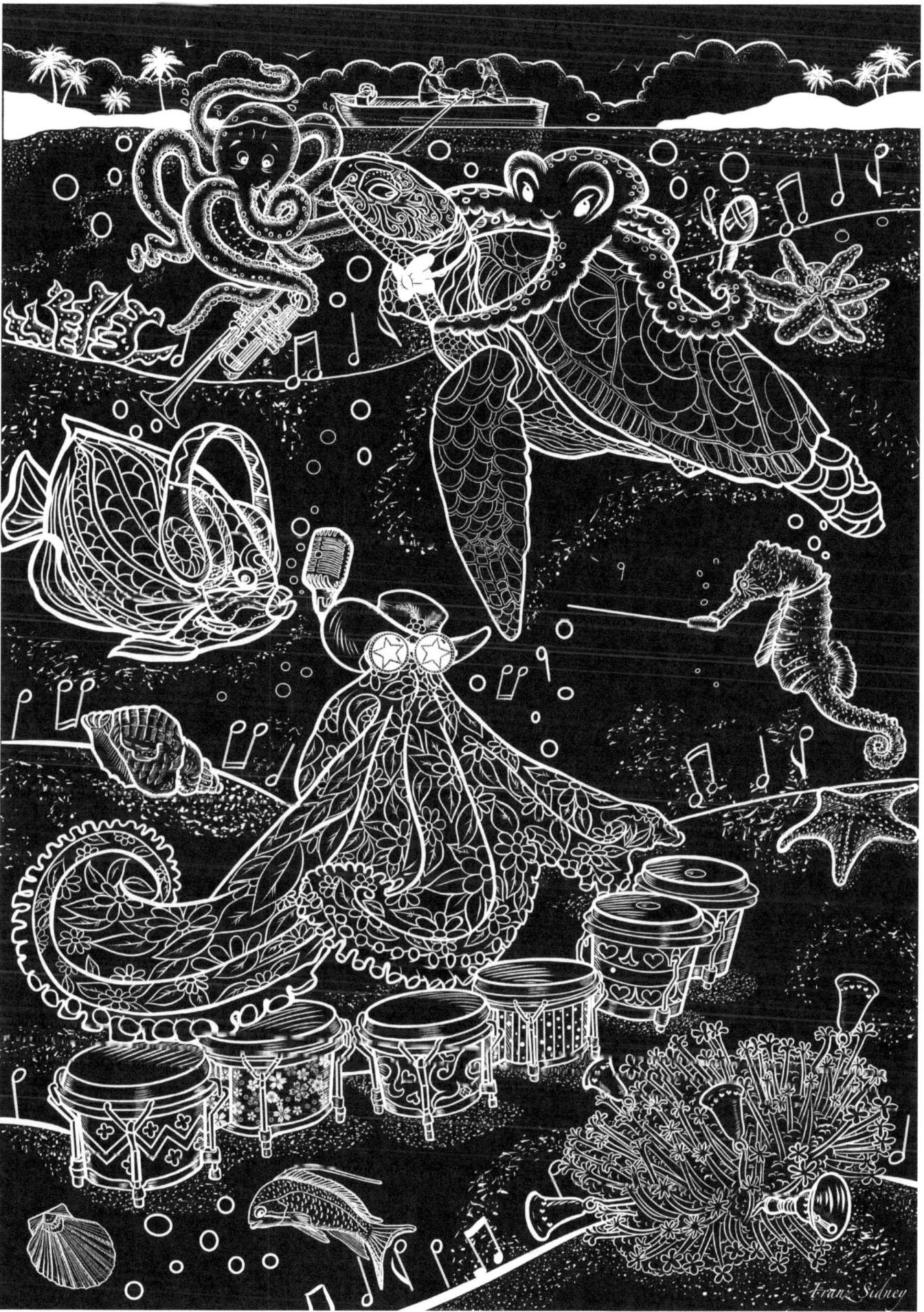

"THERE ARE NO STRANGERS HERE;
ONLY FRIENDS YOU HAVEN'T YET MET."
WILLIAM BUTLER YEATS

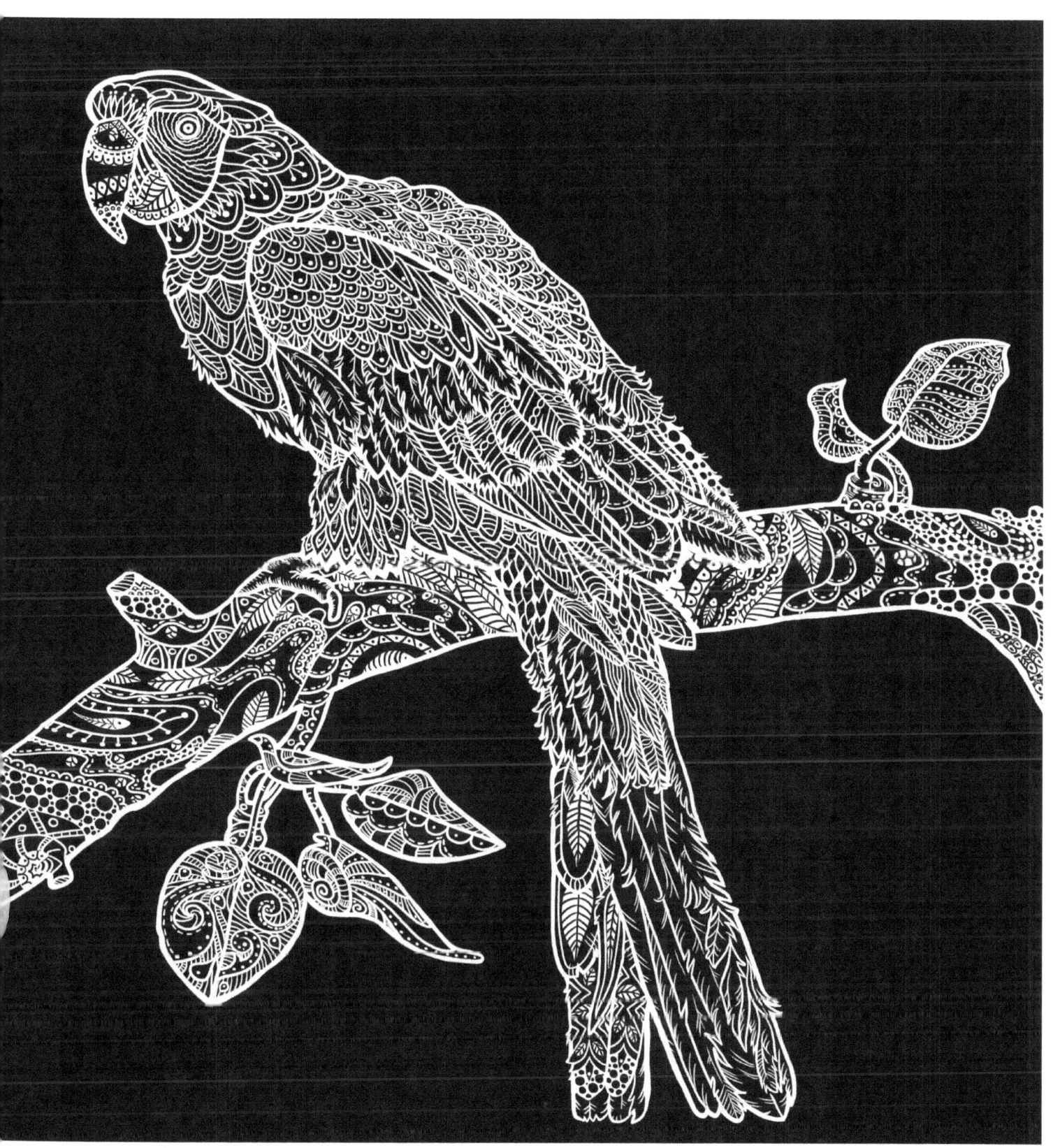

TRY YOUR PENCILS AND MARKERS HERE!

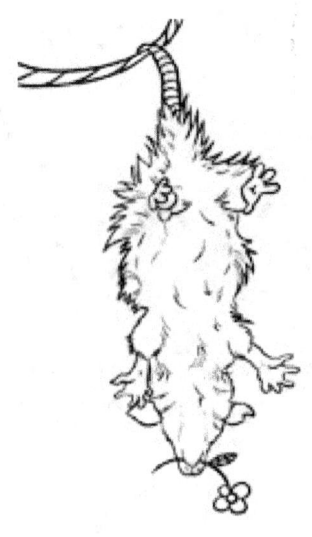

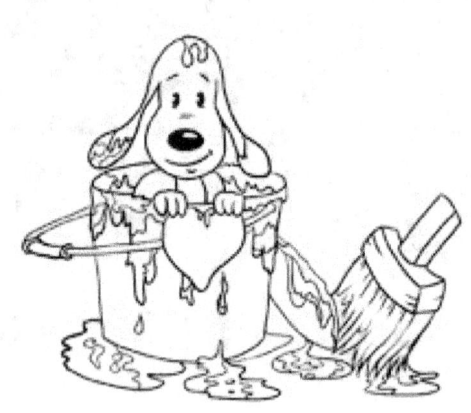

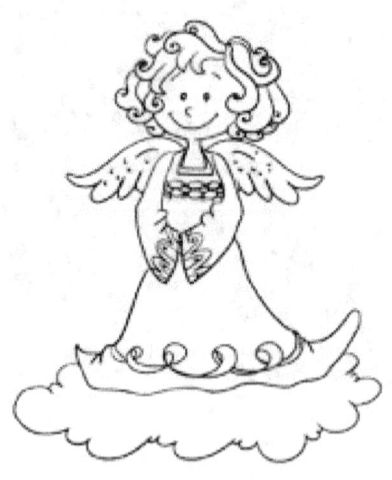

DISCOVERY

**Discovery - A colouring notebook for the easily bored
Second edition - Black and White Interior. January 2018.**

Designed and Illustrated by **Franz Sidney**
Cover art designed in collaboration with Moreno Chistè
Franz back cover photograph by
https://www.davidwoodcockphotography.co.uk

First Published in Great Britain in 2017 by Sunshine Studios

Copyright © Franz Sidney Sunshine Studios 2017
Set in Trajan Pro and Times new Roman

ISBN-13: 978-1984196200
ISBN-10: 1984196200

You can find more of Franz's art here:

https://franzsidneyart.blogspot.co.uk
https://www.zazzle.co.uk/franzsunshinestudios
https://www.redbubble.com/people/sunshinestudios

Reach your full potential with Life Coaching
www.franzsidney.com